Reflections on the Path to Wholeness
Volume 3

Going Through

BRENDA S. JACKSON, PH.D.

FOREWORD
REV. DOUW GROBLER

*Priority*ONE
publications
Detroit, Michigan, USA

Reflections on the Path to Wholeness, Volume 3: Going Through
Copyright © 2009 Brenda S. Jackson, Ph.D.

All scripture quotations, unless otherwise indicated, taken from the HOLY BIBLE, NEW INTERNATIONAL VERSION®. NIV®. Copyright© 1973, 1978, 1984 by International Bible Society. Used by permission of Zondervan. All rights reserved.

Scripture quotations marked (KJV) are taken from the HOLY BIBLE, KING JAMES VERSION (Authorized).

All poetry submissions herein are © 2000 – 2009 Brenda S. Jackson

All rights reserved. No part of this publication may be reproduced, stored in a retrieval system, or transmitted in any form or by any means – electronic, mechanical, photocopy, recording, or any other – except for brief quotations in printed reviews, without the prior permission of the publisher.

*Priority*ONE Publications
P. O. Box 725 • Farmington, MI 48332
(800) 596-4490 Nationwide Toll Free
E-mail: info@p1pubs.com
URL: http://www.p1pubs.com

ISBN 13: 978-1-933972-13-1
ISBN 10:   1-933972-13-0

Edited by Patricia A. Hicks
Cover and interior design by PriorityONE Publications

Printed in the United States of America

TABLE OF CONTENTS

Dedication and Acknowledgements 5

Foreword   Pastor Douw Grobler 6

Seminar #1   No Pain, No Gain 9

Seminar #2   Pilot Study ~ Anger & Forgiveness 33

Seminar #3   Be Angry, But Sin Not 55

Seminar #4   Lady Hawk Down 92

Seminar #5   Rejection 117

Seminar #6   Breaking Yokes 133

Seminar #7   Going Through Tough Times 157

About the Author 179

ACKNOWLEDGMENTS AND DEDICATIONS

With gladness, I acknowledge the guidance of The Holy Spirit and my success in coming through my trials by the strength of my Lord and Savior Jesus, The Christ. I thank you, PriorityONE Publications for your willingness to forego a traditional format.

This volume is dedicated to my Sorors of Alpha Kappa Alpha Sorority, especially Dr. Audrey LaSalle Brown, and Remona Ann Green, Esquire, who helped me and others go through life struggles, to Mister Solomon, who demonstrates true friendship in times of trouble, to Missionary Minetta Hare, and to Mr. Doug Grobler of Prison Fellowship South, who opened avenues of ministry to the incarcerated in South Africa.

FOREWORD

From being a policeman, tasked with enforcing the Apartheid Laws during the time of the struggle, through working as a missions pastor, caring for those very people I once persecuted, to leading a national ministry that sets itself the goal of being a reconciling community of restoration for all, thereby rehabilitating those who have offended society and assisting in their reintegration back into the community through the proclamation and demonstration of *Ubuntu* (I am because you are) and the love of God, I have witnessed pain, rejection, suffering, anger, hate, and frustration in many forms, and the capacity of the human spirit to recover, heal, and forgive, has never ceased to amaze me.

I believe that God created us in His own image, that He made us inherently good, but that with the Fall, we took on a sinful nature. I am convinced however, that the propensity to do good and the desire to be respected, liked, and loved remains within us all. In all my years working with offenders, I have never met an evil person – just nice, ordinary folk like you and me that have committed the vilest and most terrible deeds.

Of course there are those possessed, demented, and deranged, but then we need to ask ourselves: 'who are we dealing with?' Ephesians 6 is clear that our battle is not against this world, but against rulers and principalities in the spiritual realm. This is a fact, but unfortunately misunderstood and misused by many Christians to continue the process of blame shifting as they say: 'the Devil made me do it', or 'I was possessed by a spirit of this or a spirit of that', when confronted with their crimes and trespasses.

For both the victim and the offender, healing cannot commence until responsibility is taken for the right things – the offender for the choices made and the harms and consequences inflicted, and the victim for responding to the offence and that which is within his/her control. For only when we face our wounds, when we confront our sins, can we hope to recognize and accept the healing that we need.

Pain is a reality of life, in fact life is a journey of pain – from birth pains, growth pains, and the pain of young hearts broken, to the pain and discomfort that most often accompanies death, resulting in painful loss and separation. Yet, pain is not always negative or destructive. It protects the body by acting as a warning system. A friend of mine once said: I don't mind the pain – it tells me I'm alive!' Dr. Bruce Wilkinson also discusses the painful process of pruning in his book 'Secrets of the Vine' (2001), referring to our resistance to God's pruning actions in our lives. But pain is real. It hurts, it causes a decline in ability, focus, and power, and it needs to be dealt with decisively

As Christians, we often have difficulty understanding that emotions are morally neutral. They are neither good nor bad, although they are often brought about and/or result in sinful behavior.

In addition, and although central to Christ's teachings, we also struggle with the concept of forgiveness. We fail to understand that it is a journey – sometimes very long – and that the decision to forgive does not come at the end of that journey of healing, but at the very beginning.

Through the act of forgiving, a form of 'empowerment' flows from the one being forgiven to the one offering forgiveness. This is best understood if forgiveness is seen as surrendering the need to see the score settled – a turning away from revenge and hate. It is not saying: 'it's OK, it didn't hurt', or 'it doesn't matter', but taking control by choosing not to continue empowering the offender with the right to weigh us down emotionally, spiritually, and physically. It is taking control of our future, our healing, and our emotions.

The Christian imperative 'to forgive and forget' is a fallacy. God does not command us to forget as He forgets, only to forgive as He forgives. It is very difficult if not impossible for humans to forgive *and forget*. Can a mother be expected to forget her murdered child – of course not, and Christ does not expect her to. Should we in South Africa forgive one another for the atrocities committed under Apartheid – Yes – Christ commands it. Should we forget – No – that would doom us to repeating it.

We need to build better relationships through deepening our understanding, acceptance, and respect for one another by listening, caring, and demonstrating a Spirituality of reconciliation, forgiveness, and healing that transcends programs or initiatives, but manifests as a way of life.

Relationships with others can only be healthy if our relationships with ourselves and with God are healthy. If we find our identity in Christ as children created in God's image, then our value is not impacted by worldly rejection, earning capacity, or material worth. This may sound easy, but unless we daily strive to allow the facts, supported by our beliefs, lead our emotions, we will go through life on an emotional roller coaster – sometimes up, sometimes down, but never truly in control and always vulnerable to the whims of the world.

I truly believe that what Dr Jackson has accomplished with this work, is to compile a wonderful tool to facilitate the journey of healing and transformation that we all find ourselves on – the journey called life!

I sincerely pray that God will bless her with the health, energy, and vision to continue this work – benefiting so many that she will never meet, but who live in gratitude for her obedience to God's call.

Pastor Douw Grobler
Executive Director
Prison Fellowship South Africa

Chapter 1
NO PAIN, NO GAIN!

Why Does Pain Exist?
A Christian Perspective

BSJ Christian Seminars
Minister Brenda Simuel Jackson, Ph.D.
© 2008 All rights reserved.

SEMINAR OBJECTIVES

- Understand the physical and emotional aspects of pain and suffering

- Understand a probable perspective of why God's creation includes pain and suffering

- Understand differing human and spiritual responses to pain, suffering, and sorrow

MANAGING THE PAIN
© Brenda Simuel Jackson

The left side, down the thigh and sometimes the leg goes the pain, occasionally making a visit to the right.

Bending over or down causes grimaces of pain, getting up in the morning bring cries of Lord help.

Pills bring short time relief by dulling the sharpness, and the anguish of this enemy, this trouble, called pain.

Remembering the song, I will Trust in The Lord, takes my mental focus away from my discomfort, I remember Your word that says You will never leave me or forsake me, and as I go through rivers of pain, they will not sweep over me.

I remember the pharmacy in the hem of Your garment which brings me joy, I remember my weeping may endure for the night, but there is expectant joy in the morning.

I cried out, and You heard, and enabled me to rise, to walk, to carry, to sit, to travel, to endure, for now the pain is eased, and I can continue one episode at a time.

Thank You!

The Questions: Why pain? Why suffering? Why sorrow?
Romans 5:2b – 4 (NIV)

I. "And we rejoice in the hope of the glory of God. Not only so, but we rejoice in our sufferings, because we know that suffering produces perseverance; perseverance character; and character hope."

II. Pain is not the cause for rejoicing, but the process of pain is when we rejoice.
- Demonstrate the joyous life within
- Demonstrate a triumphant life
- Christians can rejoice
    - Not meaninglessly
    - God's purpose
    - Our character

III. Aspects of pain:
- What is pain?
- What is suffering?
- What is grief?
- Job 3:20-25
  "Why is light given to those in misery, and life to the bitter of soul, to those who long for death that does not come, who search for it more than for hidden treasure, who are filled with gladness and rejoice when they reach the grave? Why is life given to a man whose way is hidden, whom God has hedged in? For sighing comes to me instead of food; my groans pour out like water. What I feared has come upon me; what I dreaded has happened to me. I have no peace, no quietness; I have no rest, but only turmoil."

IV. Pain (World Book Dictionary):
- Feelings of being hurt
- Suffering
- Single or localized feeling of hurt
- Mental suffering
- Grief
- Sorrow
- Obsolete definitions are positive and negative
    - Labor
    - Work
    - Punishment
    - Penalty
- Result of physical ache of discomfort or distress (Webster)
    - Injury
    - Strain
    - Illness
- Result of emotional or mental affliction

V. Suffering results from something unpleasant and ongoing.
- Perception of suffering
    - God permits pain
    - God is with us while we suffer
    - God allows the experience of pain for our good. (Richards, 953)
- Human beings are subject to suffering all the days of this life

VI. "Grief is deep, enduring sorrow caused by the loss or impending loss of something that has strong emotional value." (Biblical Counseling, Hunt)

- In Old Testament, grief is lamenting:
    o Mental stress
    o Physical stress
    o Agony
    o Labor pains
- In New Testament, grief is from root term of pain to body or mind

VII. Prevalence of pain (Strauss, et al):
- 1986 study
- 35.5% of respondents experienced on-going chronic pain
- Occurrences increase with age
- Higher occurrence in females
- Majority (70%) in pain seek medical treatment
- Onset of condition unknown or spontaneous.

PAINFUL SITUATIONS

- Terminal illness (yours or significant other)
- Son/Daughter strung out
- Illness such as kidney failure
- Constant physical pain
- Loss of job
- Loss of material items through natural disaster
- Loss of loved ones

- Victim of theft
- Victim of violence
- Famine
- Drought
- Loss of bodily function(s)
- Loss of control of environment
- _____
- _____
- _____
- _____

Add your own circumstances of pain and suffering where you are asking why? Why me?

The Why of Pain, Suffering, Sorrow

A Warning System:

I. Theology of pain – Suffering:
- Reality of life
    - Not the era to remove pain
    - God, not man, determines the time for everlasting joy.
    - All persons, Christians and non-Christians, experience pain
    - James 1:2 (NIV) Preparation-"Consider it pure joy, my brothers, whenever you face trials of many kinds"
    - Through pain we get to know God
    - Through pain we get to know God's goodness
    - Through pain we get to know God's sovereignty
    - Where is God when it hurts? (Yancey, 120)
        - In us
        - He is transforming bad into good
    - Pain with a purpose - Amos 4:6 (NIV) - "'I gave you empty stomachs in every city and lack of bread in every town, yet you have not returned to me,' declares the Lord."
        - A world with no pain would block God's purpose for us
            - Old Testament – God took life to further His purposes
            - Stop the spread of evil
            - Jericho? Who survived?
        - Preparation of eternity with God
        - From Pain: (Yancey)
            - Pleasure
            - Good
            - Value

- From experiences of 911
    - _____ (Pleasure)
    - _____ (Good)
    - _____ (Value)
    Fill in the blanks.
- Tragedy alerts us
    - Be ready
    - There are always victims of political terrorism
- Reasons Christians suffer (Crews)
    - Fallenness – disobedience – The Adam syndrome
    - God's purpose to advance His Kingdom
    - Build character of His Saints
    - Build relationship with Christ (1 Peter 2:19, 4:15-16, 4:1,13)
    - Being conformed to the image of Christ
    - Hope: Jeremiah - "For surely I know the plans I have for you, says the Lord, plans for your welfare and not for harm, to give you a future with hope." (NRSV)
    - Redemption (Crews)
    - Suffering and salvation
        - Messiah, a man of sorrow
        - Suffered for us
        - Knows what suffering is
        - God allowed Jesus to suffer
        - Through suffering He was our vindication
        - Romans 8:28-29
        - God is found in our pain and suffering

- - - We are molded into God's image
    - Perseverance is built (Romans 5:3-4)
  - Growing through adversity (Isaiah 55:6-9) Experiencing true joy results from experiencing true pain
    - Learn dependence
      - "Valleys" take away independence, ego
      - Valleys point to The Lord
        - Depend on The Provider
        - Depend on The Protector
- Builds cooperation
- Defines necessities of life
- Teaches differences between false perceived fears and the reality of fear.
- Brings positive responses to the Gospel
- Through suffering life comes
  - Child bearing
  - Being born again (Romans 8:18-25)
- Being a test case – A real victim
  - Job
  - Suffering caused by vindictiveness of Satan
  - Suffering caused by seeking to embarrass God
- God suffers with us through the incarnate Jesus
  - Hebrew 2:18 (NRSV) - "Because He Himself was tested by what He suffered, He is able to help those who are being tested."
- Hebrew 5:8 – Learn obedience through suffering
- Intentional suffering – God's intent

- "Jesus' suffering, an expression of God's set purpose and foreknowledge. (Acts 2:23; 1 Peter 1:11)
- Intended for our salvation (1 Peter 3:18)
- God supervises the believer's suffering (1 Peter 3:8-18 - Suffering for doing good)

Summary of the Issue, Why?
Romans 8:18, 22-25 (NIV)

18. I consider that our present sufferings are not worth comparing with the glory that will be revealed in us...

22. We know that the whole creation has been groaning as in the pains of childbirth right up to the present time.

23. Not only so, but we ourselves, who have the firstfruits of the Spirit, groan inwardly as we wait eagerly for our adoption as sons [daughters], the redemption of our bodies.

Causes of Grief
- Loss
    i. A spouse
    ii. A friend
    iii. A parent
    iv. A child
    v. A pet
    vi. One's health
    vii. One's reputation
    viii. Freedom
    ix. Employment
    x. Justice
    xi. Home
    xii. Finances
    xiii. Physical abilities
    xiv. Family environment

BIBLICAL Examples of Persons in PAIN

SCRIPTURES	PERSON	THE PAIN	RESULTS
2 Kings 5	Naaman	Grief/Loss of relationships leprosy, desperate situation, pride	Followed instructions leading to healing, committed to worship the Lord only
Numbers 12	Miriam	Physical Illness She was jealous of Moses, rebuked by God, stricken with leprosy, put outside the camp, pain limited in time to 7 days	Learn a doctrinal truth, demonstrates danger of dissatisfaction with what God has for us in position. It is wrong to yearn for what The Lord has given someone else
Matthew 9:18-23; Mark 5:21-42	Jairus, Synagogue ruler	Grief and Fear His daughter was dying	He went seeking Jesus Witness to unbelievers of who He [Jesus] is when life was given back to his daughter; faith strengthened
2 Corinthians 11:23-29	Paul	Physical Pain (forty lashes) Near death several times, hunger, thirst, and no sleep	Depended on the strength of God; acknowledged personal weakness
Mark 5:21-42	Woman with Issue of Blood	Grief and Pain Loss of fellowship because of her issue, pain, loss of finances, lack of healing from physicians	Faith to Seek Jesus Touched the hem of His garment, and immediately healed.
Job 1-42	Job	Grief and Pain loss of children, loss of wealth, loss of status, loss of health, loss of respect from wife; he had a limited view of God, couldn't understand why he suffered	Job submitted to God unconditional submission, and God restored his health, wealth, and family.

BIBLICAL Examples of Persons in PAIN cont'd

SCRIPTURES	PERSON	THE PAIN	RESULTS
Genesis 37-50	Joseph, son of Jacob	<u>Emotional Oppression</u> Sold by brothers, falsely accused of rape, incarcerated for 2 years, loss of family, loss of freedom, loss of trust from employer	God's plan to preserve His people implemented, reconciliation with his family, forgiveness, start of a nation
Isaiah 38:9-20	Hezekiah	<u>Grief and Depression</u> Near death experience	Appealed to God, life extended

Suffering and Faith are a Complementary Relationship

- Because of our faith in God, we let God work things
    - According to His plan
    - According to His Grace
    - According to His Mercy
- The path of suffering can be a sacred journey (1Peter 2:21)
- Pain will turn us to God if we do not put up a struggle (Yancey, 278)
- "Catastrophe can join victim and bystander in call to repentance, as we are remined, as we are reminded that life brief." (Yancey)
- Faith will cause one not to be shaken, because suffering has fortified your faith. (Job)
- Confidence in God that He understands our pain
- Our suffering may be deemed a part of the Cross of Jesus that we carry:
    - We know God cares for us.
    - We know Jesus died for us.
- Our lifetime includes suffering, "a mere moment" in time, next to eternity.

- Our pain system was designed by God to warn us:
  - Physical problems
  - Emotional problems
  - Spiritual problems

Faith and Grief are a Complementary Relationship

- God comforts (2 Corinthians 1:3)
- The heart is open to pain (2 Corinthians 1:9)
- Keep a clear conscience of no wrong (Psalm 32:5)
- We can find the positive in the grief process (2 Corinthian 7:11)
- God will send comforters (2 Corinthians 7:6)
- We can comfort others (2 Corinthians 1:4)

Small Group Discussion Questions

1. In times of trouble are you more likely to feel God's presence or His absence? Why?
2. When you are hurt, what help have you sought? Why?
3. How does 1 Corinthians 13 apply to practical ways for suffering persons?
4. Who causes suffering? *Read Luke 13:10-16; 13:1-5; John 9:1-3; I Corinthians 11:29-30; Acts 5:1-11; 2 Corinthians 12:7-10*
5. Can you embrace?
    a. Pain
    b. Guilt
    c. Fear
    d. Loneliness
6. Can the awareness of the value of pain help you to bear the pain?
7. Is it appropriate to thank God for the absence of pain? The presence of pain? Why?

Share personal experiences of physical or emotional suffering where you found a treasure. Describe the treasures found.

Bearing The Cross of Pain
(How do we react to Pain?)

Different Professional Paradigms of Reactions:

- Westberg:
    - State of Shock – lack of belief at the circumstances[1]
    - Emotional relief – The tears
    - Depression - loneliness[2]
    - Physical distress
    - Panic – can't think straight
    - Guilt[3]
    - Sharing the feelings
    - Anger/resentment
    - Finding comfort in the grief[4]
    - Hope

- Crews - Four Perceptions of suffering:
    - Deserved
        - Personal sin
        - Source of discipline
        - Result of bad decisions
    - Avoids with hope in resurrection of life.
    - Undeserved – Job
    - Unavoidable – No control

---

[1] Should last from a few minutes to a few days; if longer requires professional help. One must work to accept the reality of the situation.
[2] In cases of loss, recognize the depression, and know it will pass.
[3] Normal guilt requires seeking forgiveness, which requires admitting the guilt.
[4] Don't get too comfortable, keep positive memories, and take your life back.

FAITH BUILDING RESPONSES

- Nurture your faith
- Entrust yourself to God (1 Peter 2:23-25)
- Do not let fear overwhelm you (1 Peter 3:14)
- Keep focus on Christ as Lord of your life (I Peter 3:15)
- Keep positive attitude (1 Peter 3:15,16)
- Keep doing what is right (1 Peter 3:16; 4:19)
- Rejoice that you follow Jesus, knowing His glory is being revealed in you (1 Peter 4:13)
- Continue to worship God, do not challenge Him as did Job
- Rely on Scripture
- Accept your reality
- Pray
- Recall the good times
- Weep
- Put the past behind, accept the present, know God is your future.
- Yancey (p. 215) - "…healthiest body is one that feels the pain of its weakest parts."
- Feel the pain (it's real)
- Develop coping skills
- Know you are building a character like Christ's
- Seek to respond as a believer in the gospel
    - God's compassion
    - God's healing
    - God's assurance
- Knowledge is good but seek love

- Keep as much control as possible – depend on Christ for strength
- Do not immobilize the Spirit – let His power overflow
- Embrace the Journey (Allender, p. 31-46)
    - Wait with expectation
    - Know that you are not alone
    - Let go and let God
    - Don't dread any moment that comes from God
    - Continually seek God

The Ultimate in Coping – Your Witness

Yancey (p. 230) says, "People who have suffered are best equipped to help,... A person crosses the final barrier of helplessness when he or she learns to use the experience of suffering itself as a means of reaching out to others."

"Willie Lou"
©2007 Brenda Simuel Jackson

"Willou," the oldest of the once living nine. Her favorite phrase, I'm fine.

"Willou," the person to know, if seeking joy, or a slight grin, in her you would find, with the words, I'm fine.

Willou," in summers past, to the State Fair, Bob-Lo, The Village, Church and Family Outings and yes the Zoo, how was it Lou? Fine!

"Willou," secrets she kept, gossip never spread, harmful news she never shared. How goes it today Lou? Just fine.

Lou and I, United Conference for Women, once all sisters attended, a time of drawing closer to God and each other, none offended. How was the trip? Fine.

"Willou," struggled quietly for ten years with the enemy disease, through it, her faith and trust was like a fresh breeze. How do you feel today Sis? Oh, I'm fine.

Thank you Sis for sharing yourself, a life of caring at its best. Hardly a complaint was heard, but prayers, and songs rose high like birds, I'm so glad I can say, Yes, You are just Fine!

BIBLICAL RESPONSES TO SUFFERING FOR RIGHTEOUSNESS
(1 Peter 3:8 - 4:2, 23, 19; 5:7)

- Live in harmony
- Be sympathetic
- Love as brothers
- Be compassionate
- Do not repay evil with evil
- Do not give insult for insult
- Keep the tongue from evil
- Keep from deceitful speech
- Do good
- Do not fear
- In your heart know Jesus
- Keep hope
- Know that you are saved through the resurrection of Jesus Christ
- Keep the attitude of Christ
- Live in the will of God
- Rejoice that you suffer with Christ
- Cast all your anxiety on Him

BIBLIOGRAPHY

Bibles

Barker, K. (Gen Ed.), (1985) *The NIV Study Bible,* Grand Rapids, MI: Zondervan,

The Holy Bible, NRSV. (2005). MA: Hendrickson, Publishers.

Books

Allender, PhD., D. (1999). *The Healing Path.* Colorado: Waterbrook Press.

Richards, L.O. (1999). *The Revell Bible Dictionary.* New Jersey: Fleming H. Revell Co.

Westberg, Granger E. (2004) *Good Grief.* 35th ed. Minneapolis, MN: Augsburg Fortress Publishers.

Yancey, Philip. (1990). *Where is God When it Hurts?* Grand Rapids, MI: Zondervan.

Articles and Tapes

Crews, PhD., F. Pain & Suffering: Helping People in a Hurting World in *Caring for People God's Way.* Course in Biblical Counseling. American Association of Christian Counselors.

Hunt, J. (2004) Grief Recovery. *Counseling Through The Bible, Vol II.* Dallas, TX: Hope For The Heart, 1-13.

Strauss, S., Simon, L., and Nicolosi, F. *The Epidermiology of Pain, An Australian Study.* University of Queensland. Retrieved 6/6/2008 (http://www.pain-education.com/ 1000089.php).

Compilations

Barnhart, C. L., Barnhart, R. Eds. (1976). *The World Book Dictionary, Vol II*. Chicago, IL: Field Enterprises Educational Corp.

Webster's Medical Dictionary. (1992). New York: PMC Publishing Co., Inc.

Chapter 2
A PILOT STUDY

A Descriptive and Correlation Analysis of the
Relationship Between Anger and Forgiveness

BSJ Christian Seminars
Minister Brenda Simuel Jackson, Ph.D.
© 2008 All rights reserved.

INTRODUCTION

What is Anger?

From a Biblical New Testament perspective, anger is revealed to be a negative state of being. According to Vine's Expository Dictionary, the Greek term used in the following passages is indicative of "…an abiding state of mind, not just an outburst," (p. 26). The Scriptures further describe an image of destructiveness to the bearer who is in this state of being:

Scripture References	State of Being
Ephesians 4:31 - NIV	"Get rid of all bitterness, and rage, anger, brawling, and slander, along with every form of malice." These qualities are said to grieve [cause to anger] the Holy Spirit. This a self destructive state.
Colossians 3:8 - NIV	"But now you must rid yourselves of all such things as these: anger, rage, malice, slander and filthy language from your lips." This is the second warning which is an indication that there is a problem with being in this state.
1 Timothy 2:8 - NIV	"I want men everywhere to lift up holy hands in prayer, without anger or disputing." This is an indication that anger is not a holy process, and especially when it is part of the act of a dispute.
James 1:19-20 – author paraphrase	"My dear brothers take note of this: Everyone should be quick to listen, slow to speak and slow to become angry, for man's anger does not bring about the righteous life that God desires."
Job 6:4	Anger is described as the poison of arrows.

Chart I – Biblical Anger

As a general descriptor, anger is a word for a negative emotion (World Book Dictionary, 1976, p. 79, World Book). The degrees of intensity of anger are seen in the words of "indignation," a more formal meaning of intense anger mixed with scorn and [may be] an indication of justifiable anger (p.79). The greatest intensity is seen in the terminology of wrath with a desire to punish.

Dennis L. Okholm in his article, "To Vent or Not To Vent?" in <u>Care For The Soul</u>, edited by Mark R. McMinn and Timothy R. Phillips (2001), defines anger as "a boiling and stirring up of wrath against one who has given injury or is thought to have done so" (p. 168). This definition has roots in Old Testament Biblical occurrences where the Hebrew term refers to burning.

Richard Fitzgibbons, a psychotherapist, in his article, "Anger and The Healing Power of Forgiveness: A Psychiatrist's view" in <u>Exploring Forgiving</u>, edited by Robert D. Enright and Joanna North, (1998), anger is a strong feeling of displeasure and antagonism aroused by a sense of injury or wrong (p. 63).

The continuum or varying degrees of the intensity of anger are seen in the Greek terminology, $\alpha\gamma\alpha\nu\alpha\kappa\tau\eta\sigma\iota\sigma$ rendered indignation in the translation of 2 Corinthians 7:11. This is in line with the definition given by World Book. This same degree of anger is shown in Matthew 20:24 (NIV, 1985), which describes how the disciples felt toward the mother of the two disciples who was seeking special favor for her sons. Intense anger was not restricted from the followers of Christ. This degree of anger was also shown by the Pharisees who were reacting against Jesus because of His healing of the sick. In line with the continuum, the term wrath, the extreme form in Greek, is shown in Romans 10:19, but has been translated as angry in many translations, and therefore g the intenseness of the meaning has been weakened.

For the purposes of this study, the working definition of anger is a cognitive of inner turmoil which prevents positive thoughts and/or intentions towards the source or cause of the emotion. The cognition may or may not present itself in negative terms, but an emotion is felt by the person.

THE ANGER SYSTEM

What are the causes of anger?

Fitzgibbons says, "Anger develops as a natural response of the failure of others to meet one's needs for love, acceptance, and justice…" (p. 64). Carter, Ph.D and Minirth, M.D., (1993), describe three causes of anger: 1) violation of a person's feelings of self-esteem or personal value, 2) the blockage from obtaining perceived needs, and 3) violation of one's personal beliefs (*The Anger Workbook*, pp 8-13). Other violations which lead to anger are the physical violation of one's being, violation trust, or a simple destruction of an aspect of one's cognitive system (forcing one to change his/her understanding or belief).

What are the characteristic cognitions which identify the presence of anger?

Joanna North, editor of *Exploring Forgiveness*, 1998, and author of *The 'Ideal' of Forgiveness: A Philosopher's Exploration*, says anger has emotional and behavioral effects such as "anxiety, nervousness, depression, suspicions and mistrustfulness" (p. 18). Anger per Fitzgibbons, has by-products of sadness, fear, as well as perceived pleasure at the expectation of revenge and of venting anger (p. 64). Just as the semantic cognition for the emotion of anger has degrees of intensity, there is a behavioral continuum of expressing anger which ranges from the extreme of withdrawing into self-pity and harboring critical thoughts to physical outbursts and attacks (Carter and Minirth, p. 4-5).

Doris Donnelly (1979), an educator at Princeton Theological Seminary, writes, "the thread that runs consistently through the issue [anger], is revenge" (p 72). Donnelly aptly describes how a person becomes a victim of their anger:

"When I am hurt, physically, or spiritually, my wounds have power over me, they tell me what I can or can't do. And when I am wounded spiritually… I am likewise led by the power of the memories, and those experiences (p. 72)."

Marietta Jaeger in her article, *The Power and Reality of Forgiveness: Forgiving the Murder of One's Child* (1998), agrees with Donnelly and says that the evidence of deep anger is the desire for revenge.

Although there is no concrete evidence that the following violent acts resulted from anger, it is hypothesized that a negative emotion similar to anger was a factor in the 598 stabbing and 560 shooting cases in the workplaces of the United States occurring between July, 1992, and July 1993, reported from Northwestern National Line Insurance Company in 1993, and are primary examples of the destructive possibilities of anger. Jaeger describes the extreme characteristics of anger, "a willingness to kill the perpetrator,… I believe I could have done so with my bare hands, and a big smile" (p. 10).

"Anger can become a part of one's personality, and when that happens, the person can no longer find peace" (Carter & Minirth, p.17).

Ephesians 4:26-32 emphasizes as does Chart I, that from anger comes vengeance, profanity, slander, the desire to harm, bitterness in one's outlook to life, wrath, and unforgiveness.

When we look at the lives of persons in Scripture, Jonah can be described as the "Angry Messenger." Jonah was consumed by his "hatred of Ninevah" (Assyria). He was a man forced to do a good action for a nation to which he was not able to extend forgiveness. It was the Assyrian Empire which destroyed the Northern Kingdom of Israel. Jonah had only resentment. He received no joy or peace at the salvation of Ninevah. Although Ninvah had the victory, Jonah remained a victim of his own anger (Book of Jonah).

ANGER AND FORGIVENESS

What is the treatment and cure for victims of their own anger?

> The Rev. Walter Everett's shock at the murder of his son, 24-year old Scott, turned to rage when the killer plea-bargained his way to a five-year sentence. When the killer, a drug addict named Michael Carlucci, was sentenced, he said that although they must sound like empty words to the Everetts, he was sorry for what he had done.
>
> On the anniversary of his son's death, Everett, a United Methodist Minister, composed a letter to Carlucci in which he talked of his family's suffering. And then he wrote: 'Although words seems so trivial in some ways, I do accept your apology, and, as hard as these words are to write, I add: I forgive you.' ...I felt a burden lifted from my shoulders. ...It was the beginning of healing for me." (Americans Discover Power of Forgiveness, The Detroit News, December 21, 1997).

According to this News article, the Reverend Everett received therapeutic value in forgiving. Is forgiving the psychotherapy for anger? Before exploring this question, we will look at an example the concept of forgiveness.

What is Forgiveness?

In John 8:1-11, the encounter of Jesus with the adulterous woman is told, and what is learned is that the wrongdoer does not need to seek forgiveness to receive forgiveness. The woman had been accused and found guilty (v 3-5), and the only time she speaks is when Jesus asks the question (v 10), "...Woman where are they? Did no one condemn you?" She said (v 11), "No one, Lord." Jesus was the initiator of forgiveness (Donnelly, p. 115) when He said, "Neither do I condemn you; go your way..." (NASB).

Forgiveness from a Biblical view is a voluntary act. Biblical forgiveness does not negate a wrong act; it is a release from a wrong act, a setting free. In the Hebrew and Greek to forgive means "...<u>to cover</u> or atone... to carry or to take away...to pardon...to be gracious...to dismiss or send away... remission..." (Richards, 1990, p. 396). Vine reminds us that forgiveness in the Greek is also the term for grace, unconditional favor (1985), as stated in Romans 4:7. Forgiving is the cancellation of a debt (Richards, 1990), and/or the suspension of a deserved penalty (Vines et al).

There is an emotional component to forgiveness. Fitzgibbons says forgiving is "...abandoning one's angry feelings and thoughts..." (p. 65). There is agreement between the World Book, Enright, and North that to forgive is to give up the wish to punish or to get even. In forgiving, the right to resentment is relinquished, negative judgment is given up, and indifferent behavior toward one who unjustly injured is reduced. An unlikely attitude which emerges is compassion and love (Enright, et al. p. 47). North states that forgiveness is a volitional change of attitude, and therefore, the effects are the replacement of bitterness and anger with compassion and affection (p. 20).

Forgiveness is therefore the intentional act and mental releasing of a person from negative thoughts and desires of revenge and/or punishment, and the replacement of the negative cognition with a positive cognition. Etymologically, to forgive is 'to give' (Donnelly, p. 58). As our Father gave when we received our pardon and life, to forgive is to give another life (see the Prodigal Son, Luke 15:11-32).

Forgiveness and Spirituality

The cornerstone of the Christian doctrine is that God's forgiveness, His Grace (Ephesians 1:7), is because Jesus Christ turned away God's wrath. Christ atoned, covered our sin (Ephesians 2:3; 1 John 2:2, 4:10). Forgiveness cancels any debt owed (Ephesians 2:13-14). Joanna North uses this Biblical truth as the foundation of the union between the Spirit and forgiveness which can change a person. She describes a spiritual aspect of the human being "...in which yearnings, hopes, and fears are expressed and experienced. Forgiveness is closely allied to this spiritual component of our nature" (p.17). This is a recognition that the human being is more than material matter. She states that in her personal belief system, forgiveness as a therapy tool transcends any denominational belief system.

In the philosophical and theological views, the capacity for moral actions provides the ability to forgive. This ability is a part of the spiritual "stuff" of man. This spiritual is the new creature of the believer (2 Corinthian 5:17), and is of the fruit of the Spirit as described in Galatians 5:22-23.

Forgiveness a Therapeutic Tool

If forgiveness can be used as a tool of psychotherapy, what would be the results of forgiving? When forgiveness is freely given, there is a change in the relationship between the wrongdoer and the person giving the forgiveness (North, 1987, p. 500). The forgiving increases the psyche of the self by ending any distortions in one's cognitive perception caused by prevailing thoughts of revenge, or negative thoughts of self. Joanna North reports how a victim of an assault had an increase in her perception of her value as a person after she forgave her attacker (p. 19). Margaret Halmgren reports a similar result in indicating that there was a direct relation between her self respect and her forgiving her wrongdoer (see North, 19).

The therapeutic value of forgiving has been witnessed by Fitzgibbons in his psychotherapy practice, as he has witnessed its healing power. He writes how he has seen compassion replace anger and that a type of love has developed for the wrongdoer by the injured party (Fitzgibbons, p. 69). Further, emotional pain is lessened, and the "degree of sadness, hopelessness, and/or despair seems to heal" (p. 67). Enright describes how his patient indicated a state of being liberated, and how the past no longer determined or defined the present (p. 135). I agree with Wilmot and Hocker (2001) that when conflict is resolved, mental health is improved (p. 3). They report that studies from the National Institute of Mental Health support this conclusion in areas of conflict management and interpersonal therapy. Interpersonal forgiveness is a tool of managing inner personal conflict. Forgiveness is a therapeutic tool and has been used effectively with children, adolescents, and adults (Fitzgibbons, p. 71). He reports:

> "…the psychotherapeutic uses of forgiveness have resulted in a significant diminishment in the emotional, mental, and physical suffering in our clients and have contributed to successful reconciliation in a variety of relationships" (p. 63).

Enright, North, Fitzgibbons, Carter, and Minirth, report similar results in the processes leading to the ability to forgive. Commonalities include personal honesty in recognizing the existing pain of anger, rage, hatred; and not to deny their existence, a willingness to recognize a desire for justice or revenge, the ability to look out from self and to recognize moral or religious duty to forgive, the separation of the wrongful act from the wrong doer, and the release of the demand for repayment. There is a transformation from negative feelings to positive emotions.

North does point out that in "horrific" crimes, where wrong is of such a magnitude so as to defy understanding, there may be an inability to forgive (p. 27).

Empirical Pilot

Following is a Descriptive Comparative and Correlation Analysis as the initial phase in a study to empirically assess the relationship between felt anger and the behavior of forgiving. The pilot was conducted from April 9, 2002 when the initial instruments were e-mailed and/or given to respondents, through April 15, 2002, when the last instrument was distributed to seminary respondents. During this period, instruments were also distributed via the U.S. mail.

There were two groups of respondents in the pilot. Group one (1) respondents were selected based on the knowledge that the respondents had experienced situations that could produce sustained anger in persons such as physical abuse or unfairly losing a job. The participants were selected from work settings, church settings, and seminary class.

Completed instruments were returned anonymously in 80% of the returns. Group two (2) respondents were randomly selected in that there was no knowledge of the respondents having experienced situations which could produce sustained anger. This group was a class of undergraduate and graduate students at a local University extension site.

The instrument (an original document) was used for the collection of data and is not a validated instrument. The data from the pilot will be used to validate portions of the instrument and to test its reliability. Due to the nature of the data, descriptive, nonparametric tests of significance will be used at a future date for further analysis.

There are four types of variables in the design of the investigation:

- the classification variables – describing properties of the population measured

- the dependent variables – the effects of anger and forgiveness

- the independent variables – the cause of anger, and the behavior of forgiving

- the intervening variables of faith – belief in the Bible, and prayer (See Appendix II for a copy of the test instrument.)

In the future, a complete analysis will provide statistical correlations between the variables, as well as between the two different groups. The pilot groups consist of 46 respondents, 17 persons in group 1 and 29 persons in group 2.

The return rate of the respondents was 77%; 46 out of 65 instruments were returned completed either in part or fully.

Chart two provides an overview of the classification variables and demonstrates the differences and similarities between the two groups.

Chart three, "The Relationship of the Dependent Variable, Anger, to the Independent Variable (Cause of Anger)" demonstrates a positive relationship between betrayal of trust, being lied about, having one's character slandered, theft, cheated on, psychological abuse and the felt anger of resentment, hurt, sadness, and the desire for revenge in group I.

Only the top six causes are sited above, although all causes listed received a positive response from at least four of the respondents. Only the top four effects are presented although all nine effects received at least three positive responses from group 1.

In group 2, being lied about, having one's trust betrayed, psychological abuse, being cheated on, theft, and physical abuse received the highest number of responses as a cause of anger. The effects of the anger were sadness, hurt, resentment, and hatred.

In both groups, issues related to trust are the greatest cause of sustained anger; resentment, hurt, and sadness are the three greatest anger responses in both groups. 69% of all the respondents were female; 76% of group 1 was female and 66% of group 2 was female. Gender may be related to the type of response demonstrating anger.

Chart four, "The Relationship of the Dependent Variable (Releasing Anger) and the Independent Variable (Forgiving); demonstrates a positive relation between forgiving and a change in attitude which could be defined as a spiritual healing. The responses reported in group 1 after the act of forgiving are release, relief, peace, calmness, and no fear. These were the top five responses. The respondents in group 2 reported that after the act of forgiving there was release, relief, calmness, peace, and no fear. The top five responses in group 2 are the same as those reported in group 1. Although not in the top five for either group, concern for the wrongdoer ranked 7th out of 10 for group 1 respondents, and empathy and compassion ranked 6th and 7th respectively for group 2. Although not proof of a cause and effect relationship, there does appear to be support for the hypothesis that a positive relationship exists between healing from anger and the act of forgiving the wrongdoer.

It is further noted that in group one 82% were Christian and 69% in group two were Christian. In group one 88% believed in the inerrancy of the Bible, and 79% in group two did also.

59% of respondents in group one reported prayer was used to cope with the problem prior to forgiving, and 10% of group two resorted to prayer.

Age did not appear to be a significant factor in the type of healing which resulted from forgiving, nor was it a factor in the type of anger felt after its initiation. Level of education does not appear to be a significant factor in the top five healing responses of forgiving.

Ethnic background was not a factor between the two groups in the responses to anger or the responses to forgiveness. Group one consisted of 76% African-American and 12% Caucasian, and group two consisted of 48% Caucasian and 17% African -American.

It does appear that the act of forgiving is of therapeutic value in psychotherapy for persons suffering from the effect of anger as defined in this study. It is noted that the population was primarily Christian. An extension of the pilot would include a more diverse religious pool.

APPENDIX
I & II

For purposes of this study, anger is defined as, "a boiling and stirring up of displeasure, antagonism, rage against one or against others who have given wrongful injury or is thought to have injured you, physically, mentally, and or spiritually. (*The Psychology of Interpersonal Forgiveness*, by Robert D. Enright, Suzanne Freedman, and Julio Rique in *Exploring Forgiveness* edited by Robert D. Enright and Joanna North, eds., University of Wisconsin Press, 1998, and *To Vent or Not to Vent?* By Dennis Okholm in *Care for the Soul,* Intervarsity Press, 168). Forgiving is defined as the voluntary act of giving up the right to "resentment, negative judgment, or revenge toward the wrong doer(s) who unjustly injured you. (Ibid.)

1. Causes of Anger – Please circle those acts of wrongdoers of which you were the victim or a injured party. (Note: These events are to be real situations.)

    a. Unfairly lost a job
    b. Lied about
    c. Physically abused
    d. Psychologically abused
    e. Sexually abused
    f. Loved one intentionally injured or murdered
    g. Theft
    h. Raped
    i. Character slandered
    j. Trust betrayed
    k. Cheated on
    l. Financial ruin
    m. Other _____

2. Have you forgiven at least one wrong doer? Yes____ No ____

3. If you answered yes to number 2, which of the causes of anger did you forgive? _____

   If you answered No to number 2, please go to Demographic information.

4. At the time of the wrongful act cited in number 3, which of the following emotions do you remember feeling?

   a. Hatred
   b. Resentment
   c. Emptiness
   d. Fear
   e. Wrath
   f. Sadness
   g. Desire to do bodily harm
   h. Desire for revenge
   i. Hurt
   j. Cannot describe

5. What actions did you take to reduce the emotions cited in Number 4? _____
   _____
   _____
   _____
   _____

6. How much time elapsed before you forgave the wrong doer?
   _____
   _____

_____

_____

7. The following is a list of emotional attitudes regarding your personal perception of how you felt after forgiving the wrong doer for the act cited in number 3. Check the attitudes which best describe your perception of how you felt.

Attitudes	Strongly felt	Felt somewhat	Did not feel
Compassion			
Calmness			
Catharsis of emotions			
Concern for the wrong doer			
Empathy			
Joy			
Fear			
Peace			
Relief			
Release			

DEMOGRAPHIC INFORMATION:

Circle one:

1. Sex: 1 = male 2 = female
2. Marital Status: 1 = married   2 = single   3 = divorced
                     4 = widow/widower   5 = separated
3. Age: 1 = 0-25 2 = 26-40   3 = 41-55
                     4 = 56-68   5 = 68+
4. State your ethnic heritage:
5. What is your religious faith?
6. Do you believe in the truth of the Bible?   ☐ Yes   ☐ No

~ 48 ~

7. Education - Check one:
   - ☐ 0 – High School or equivalent
   - ☐ Some College
   - ☐ College Degree
   - ☐ Graduate Degree

DESCRIPTION OF CLASSIFICATION VARIABLES

Gender	Female	13	19	32	0.696
	Male	2	9	11	0.239
	Unanswered	2	1	3	0.065
	Totals	17	29	46	100%
Marital Status	Married	8	14	22	0.478
	Single	1	8	9	0.196
	divorced	5	4	9	0.196
	widow/widower	2	1	3	0.065
	Separated	0	0	0	0.000
	Unanswered	1	2	3	0.065
	Totals	17	29	46	1.000
Age	"0-25"	0	3	3	0.0652
	"26-40"	2	12	14	0.3043
	"41-55"	6	10	16	0.3478
	"56-68"	6	1	7	0.1522
	"68+"	2	0	2	0.0435
	Unanswered	1	3	4	0.0870
	Totals	17	29	46	1.0000
Ethnic Heritage/ Racial Designation (Categories defined as per US Census)	American Born	14	14	28	0.609
	Non-American Born	1	6	7	0.152
	Unanswered	2	9	11	0.239
	Totals	17	29	46	1.000
	African American	13	5	18	0.391
	Asian Pacific Islander	0	2	2	0.043
	Caucasian	2	14	16	0.348
	Hispanic	0	0	0	0.000
	Native Born Indian/Alaskan	0	0	0	0.000
	Unanswered	2	8	10	0.217

	Totals	17	29	46	1.000
Religious Faith	Christian	14	20	34	0.739
	Non-Christian	0	1	1	0.022
	None	0	1	1	0.022
	Unanswered	3	7	10	0.217
	Totals	17	29	46	1.000
Belief in The Truth of The Bible	Yes	15	23	38	0.826
	No	1	3	4	0.087
	Unanswered	1	3	4	0.087
	Totals	17	29	46	1.000
Education	0 -HS or Equivalent	3	1	4	0.087
	Some College	6	9	15	0.326
	College Degree	2	15	17	0.370
	Graduate Degree	5	3	8	0.174
	Unanswered	1	1	2	0.043
	Totals	17	29	46	1.000

BIBLIOGRAPHY

Bibles

Barker, K. (Gen.Ed.)/ (1985) *The NIV Study Bible.* Grand Rapids, MI: Zondervan Bible Publishers.

Radamacher, E. Th.D., Allen, Ronald B. Th.D. and House, H. Wayne, Th.D. J.D., eds. (1997) *The Nelson Study Bible NKJV.* Nashville, TN: Thomas Nelson Publishers.

Scofield, C.I., D.D. (1967) *The New Scofield Study Bible NKJV.* Nashville, TN: Thomas Nelson Publishers.

Books

Carter, Ph.D., L. and Minirth, M.D., F. (1993). *The Anger Workbook.* Nashville, TN: Thomas Nelson Publishers.

Carter, Ph.D., L. and Minirth, M.D., F. (1997). *The Choosing to Forgive Workbook.* Nashville, TN: Thomas Nelson Publishers.

Donnelly, D. (1979). *Learning To Forgive.* New York: Macmillan Publishing Co.

Enright, R. D. and North, J. Eds. (1998). *Exploring Forgiveness.* Madison, WI: University of Wisconsin Press.

Ferguson, G. A. (1971). *Statistical Analysis in Psychology & Education.* (3rd ed.). New York: McGraw-Hill Book Company.

Perschbacker, W. ed. (1990). *The New Analytical Greek Lexicon.* Peabody, MA: Hendrickson Publishers.

Richards, Ph.D., L. (1990). *The Revell Bible Dictionary.* New Jersey: Fleming H. Revell Co.

Vine, W.E., Unger, M. F., and White Jr., W. Eds. (1985) *Vine's Complete Expository Dictionary of Old and New Testament Words*. Nashville, TN: Thomas Nelson Publishers.

Wilmot Ph.D., W.W. and Hocker Ph.D., J. L. (2001). *Interpersonal Conflict*. (6th ed.). New York: McGraw-Hill Book Company.

Articles

McMinn, M. R., Okholm, D.L., and Phillips, T.R. (Eds.). (2001). "To Vent or Not To Vent?' What Contemporary Psychology Can Learn from Ascetic Theology About Anger. *Care For The Soul*, Illinois: Intervarsity Press 164-186.

David Briggs, Associated Press "Americans Discover Power of Forgiveness." p. 13A. The Detroit News. (December 21, 1997).

Chapter 3
BE ANGRY SIN NOT

Ephesians 4:26-31

Be angry but do not sin; do not let the sun go down on your anger, and do not make room for the devil. Thieves must give up stealing; rather let them labor and work honestly with their own hands, so as to have something to share with the needy. Let no evil talk come out of your mouths, but only what is useful for building up, as there is need, so that your words may give grace t those who hear. And do not grieve the Holy Sprit of God, with which you were marked with a seal for the day of redemption. Put away all bitterness, and wrath and anger and wrangling and slander, together with all malice, and be kind to one another, tenderhearted, forgiving one another, as God in Christ as forgiven you.

SEMINAR OBJECTIVES

- Understand what is anger
- Gain insight on how to control anger
- Understand the Biblical perspective of anger
- Know the difference between being a peacemaker and a peacekeeper
- Learn how to listen
- Recognize that forgiveness leads to peace
- See the Scriptural approach to problem- solving
- View different methods of conflict resolution

BE ANGRY BUT SIN NOT
© Brenda Simuel Jackson

Be angry but sin not when called out of your name.

Be angry but sin not when lies destroy your chance at fame.

Be angry but sin not when family turn away, rejecting your love.

Be angry but sin not for your Love comes from above.

Be angry but sin not when someone forgets not your past.

Be angry but sin not for you have a future that will last.

Be angry but sin not when doors are shut in your face.

Be angry but sin not Jesus opens doors, wait do not haste.

He bore all our sins, paid all our debt, forgiveness He gave, so to anger we will not be slaves.

ANGER SYNONYMS
- Impatience
- Bitterness
- Jealousy
- Grief/Mourning
- Rage
- Self-righteousness
- Loss of control
- Distress
- Denial
- Acquiesce

Descriptive Scriptural Definitions of Anger

What is Anger?
- A burning sensation in the throat
- Rage and pain
- Spittle
- Poison
- Heat
- Wrath
- Bitter Spirit

Anger Impacts:
- The Spirit
- The Mind
- The Body

SCRIPTURAL ANGER

SCRIPTURE	ANGER CONTEXT	ANGER IMPACT	PERSONAL EFFECT
Hosea 7:5	Anger is fever of wine	Being as drunk	
Job 6:4	Anger is poison of arrows	God's anger against Job	
Genesis 27:44-47	Jacob flees from his brother	Esau had rage against his brother	Opens way for Satan's control
Proverbs 6:34	Jealousy	Causes fury	Might take revenge
Ezekiel 3:14	Ezekiel's call; He knows God's righteous anger	He is bitter in spirit with Israel	Failure to love as Christ loves
Provers 12:16; 17:25; 21:19	Quick anger; foolishness	Bitter, hard to live with	Critical thoughts, problems in communication
Ecclesiastes 1:18, 2:23, 7:3, 11:10; Job 5:2	Grief and loss	Sorrow, pain, resentment	Mental tensions, refusal to admit personal weaknesses; inability to forgive
Genesis 30:1-2	Rachel is jealous of her sister who has given birth	Jacob is angry	Envy kills a relationship
2 Kings 4:27; Job 27:2; Proverbs 14:10; Genesis 26:35	Shunammite woman bitter over death of son; Esau grieves his parents by his choice of wives	Spiritual distress, no joy because heart is angry	Loss of joy and peace

Definition of Anger:
- An attitude
- A negative emotion
- A reaction
- A way of thinking

Three Basic Facets of Scriptural Anger:

Divine Anger – Wrath of God
- Judgment
- God's righteous anger against sin
- Holy indignation
- Anger that expresses divine love, as Jesus, The Christ took God's wrath for us
- Can your anger be divine? Why? Why not?

Human indignation often accompanied with revenge – inward feelings
- Leads to violent behavior (Luke 4:28-29)
- The self-seeking (Romans 2:8)
- Sinful fits of rage (Galatians 5:19-20)
- Those not walking in the Spirit (Romans 8:1)

A Clamour – condition of the mind which governs passions:
- This anger governs speech
    - Unrighteous speech
    - Character assassination (Matthew 5:22)
- Anger that grieves the Holy Spirit (Ephesians 4:30-31)
    - Bitterness
    - Rage

Evaluate the anger emotion:

Ask, "Why am I angry?"
- Reaction to a personal (physical, mental, or emotional) attack
- Attack on my personal worth of who I am.
    - Feelings of rejection
    - Feelings of being invalidated
    - Feelings of devaluation
- Unmet needs
    - Material
    - Mental
    - Spiritual
- Differences in philosophy and/or doctrine
    - Disharmony with how I/others think
    - Threatened by how others think
- Discouragement
- Wrongs not made right
- Pride

Recognize Anger Self Assessment:
(adapted from The Anger Work Book, Carter & Minert)

- I am frequently impatient
- I nurture critical thoughts
- In my displeasure, I may shut down or withdraw
- I am annoyed when others do not comprehend my needs.
- I feel frustrated when others have fewer struggles than I do
- I have a hard time accepting persons who do not admit their weaknesses
- I do not forget when someone does me wrong
- When someone confronts me from an uninformed position I am thinking of my rebuttal
- How angry are you?
- Did you have earlier perceptions of your anger?

Do I have the right to be angry?:

Is my anger hypocritical?

- A hypocrite says one thing but does another (Matthew 23:3)
- A hypocrite tells others what they should do, but they are not willing to give assistance (Matthew 23:4)
- A hypocrite wants to be seen (Matthew 23: 5)
- A hypocrite wants others to acknowledge them as superior (Matthew 23:6-7)

Is my anger justified or am I being self-righteous?

- Am I operating from truth?
- Am I accepting my responsibilities?
- Am I seeking respect?

- Am I impatient over others incompetence?

Hypocritical Anger:
- Seeking self-righteousness – human judging
- Anger because of unmet needs
- Anger because of self-concern

> "Do not judge, or you too will be judged. For in the same way you judge others, you will be judged, and with the measure you use, it will be measured to you. Why do you look at the speck of sawdust in your brother's eye and pay no attention to the plank in your own eye? How can you say to your brother, 'Let me take the speck out of your eye,' when all the time there is a plank in your eye? You hypocrite, first take the plank our of your own eye, and then you will see clearly to remove the speck from your brother's eye." Matthew 7:1-5 NIV

ANGER as an emotion is not a sin:
- Reasons for anger may be sinful
- Behavior of anger may be sinful

RESULTS OF ANGER
Ephesians 4:26-32

RESULTS OF ANGER	OPPORTUNITIES FOR LOVE
• Anger can lead to vengeance	• Let anger lead to truth
• Anger can lead to the use of profanity	• Let anger lead to honest work
• Anger can lead to slander	• Let anger lead t sharing with those in need
• Anger can lead to the desire to harm others	• Let anger bring wholesome speech
• Anger can lead to bitterness	• Let anger lead to kindness
• Anger can cause rash speech	• Let anger lead to forgiveness
• Anger can lead to wrath	• Let anger result in planned responses
• Anger can cause unforgiveness	• Let anger produce patience
	• Let anger cause seeking peace
	• Let anger cause seeking unity

Group Exercise:
Description of my anger:

Description of the results of my anger:

Did I take the opportunity to demonstrate love? ☐Yes   ☐No

ANGER, The Devil's Delight
Ephesians 4:26-31

I. Anger can block God's gifts:
   A. Gift of mercy
   B. Gift of grace
   C. Gift of peace

II. Portraits of Anger:
   A. Saul, 1 Samuel 18:6-12, 31:1-13
      1. Jealousy another form of anger
      2. Tried to kill David
      3. Fear of David as he knew the Lord was with David
      4. Committed suicide and never reconciled to God or David
   B. Absalom, 2 Samuel 13:1-15:12, 18:1-17
      1. Anger led to internal bitterness and hatred
      2. Anger led to the inability to forgive
      3. Killed his half brother
      4. Conspired against his father, David
      5. Was killed without reconciliation
   C. Herod the King, Matthew 2:16-17
      1. Angry with the Magi
      2. Gave orders to kill all boys two years of age and under
      3. Died never receiving reconciliation or meeting the only One able to give him salvation and the real kingdom
   D. Thief on the Cross, (Luke 23:38-43)
      1. In his frustration while dying, he hurled insults at Christ
      2. Lost the opportunity for salvation and peace
      3. Lost the opportunity for restoration and reconciliation

Anger and Battering

I. Cameo Portrait of a Batterer:

Spiritually		Psychologically	Physically
Scriptures	Characteristics	Low tolerance for frustration, low tolerance for stress	Abuses Alcohol
Psalm 32: 3-4	Failure to be honest and admit past violence	Does not acknowledge emotions	Uses threatening behavior (looks and gestures)
Job 33: 31-33	Does not see from God's perspective	Seeks power and control	Uses abusive language
Psalm 6:6-8	Does not know own Spiritual power and personal worth	Has low self esteem and unrealistic goals	
Psalm 119: 165-6	Does not obey God	Is extremely jealous and possessive	
Job 27:9-10; Psalm 10:1	Does not trust the Lord		
Psalm 37:39	Is not seeking God's forgiveness and salvation		

II. Discussion for the Batterer

A. Man has control without violence

B. Genesis 1:26-28 says, "Then God said, 'Let Us make man in our image, in our likeness, and let them rule over the fish of the sea and the birds of the air, over the livestock, over all the earth and over all the creatures that move along the ground.

C. Why treat others as if you are superior? Matthew 5:22b, "…Anyone who says to his brother, 'RACA,' is answerable to the Sanhedrin. But anyone who says, 'You fool!' will be in danger of the fire of hell." (NIV)

D. Genesis 1:26-28 says, "let them," male and female rule together over the earth.

E. How are your parenting/spousal skills?
   1. Ephesians 5:25–33, 6:4
   2. "Husbands, love your wives just as Christ loved the Church and gave himself up for her…" (NIV)
   3. Husband ought to love their wives as their own bodies, he who loves his wife loves himself."
   4. "…the two become one flesh".
   5. "However, each one of you also must love his wife as he loves himself and the wife must respect her husband
      a. Share responsibilities
      b. Make decisions together
      c. Make sure both benefit from decisions reached
   6. "Fathers, do not exasperate your children; instead bring them up in the training and instruction of the Lord."
   7. 1 Peter 3:7 – Husbands in the same way be considerate as you live with your wives, and treat them with respect as the weaker partner and as heirs with you of the gracious gift of life, so that nothing will hinder your prayers.
F. Submission is a reciprocal command, Ephesians 5:21, "Submit to one another out of reverence for Christ.
G. During periods of separation and marital issues pray! (1 Corinthians 7:5; Ephesians 6:18)

ABUSE
Biblical Examples

Biblical Accounts of Abuse	Scripture	Circumstances and Perpetuators	Justification	Role of the Believing Community
In Battle	1 Samuel 31:4,9	Saul has been wounded in battle and is seeking for his armor bearer to kill him to prevent the enemy from killing him and making sport [abusing] his body, such as cutting off the head. The Hebrew term for this abuse means humiliation.	The customs of victors; practice of evil deeds	Provide proper burial
	Judges 20:45	Gleaning men in battle by cutting them down with the sword as in the defeat of the Benjamites.		
Rape of a woman	Judges 19:25	A Levite's concubine (secondary wife), was continuously abused, **Hebrew term here means raped,** causing death in order to save the Levite from homosexual attack [rape of the man].	Hospitality was critical in ancient times, the person extending hospitality was responsible for the safety of the guest, the Levites.	The Israelites went to war against the Benjamites who refused to punish the perpetrators of the deed.
Crucifixion of Jesus Christ	Matthew 27:27-44; Luke 22:63-23:43	Beaten with leather whip containing pieces of metal to tear the skin, knocked in the head several times, crowned with thorns going inch deep into the scalp, nailed to a cross, couldn't use muscles to breathe, public shame, humiliation, degradation, made sport of by soldiers. The perpetuators: Sanhedrin, soldiers	None; Universal Sin	Some went into hiding, Others gathered, and became leaders within the Christian Faith

(Remember whose place Jesus took!)

POSITIVE OBJECTIVES OF ANGER

FORGIVENESS:
- Old Testament definition
    - To cover (as in a sacrifice), Leviticus 16
    - To appease
    - To make atonement
    - Genesis 50:17, Psalm 4:5-6
        - Cast away
        - To lift from
        - To carry from
    - Pardon to sinners (Psalm 32:1-5)
- New Testament forgiving is receiving **unmerited favor**
    - Matthew 18:21-27 How many times to forgive?
        - To send forth
        - To send away
        - To remit
        - To settle debts
    - Forgive has the meaning of a debt/sin
    - Forgive in Matthew 9:2,5,6 sins are blotted out
    - Forgive in Luke 6:37 is to release, to dismiss
    - Forgive in 1 Peter 4:8 is to remove from sight
- Relationship between forgiveness and salvation (Romans 5:9, 15-19, 8:15-17; John 3:16-17; Ephesians 2:7)
    - Salvation, the work of God to release man from sinful state
    - Salvation releases man from judgment of eternal damnation
    - Salvation is being rescued

DIVINE FORGIVENESS:
- Divine forgiveness received through belief in Jesus Christ
    - God provides the forgiveness
    - Man believes the Gospel of Jesus Christ
    - Man confesses Christ and repents of sins
- The need for Divine forgiveness is not from the actions of man.
    - Universality of sin is the result of Adam's disobedience (Romans 5:12, 16, 19; Galatians 3:10; Ephesians 2:1-3)
    - Man has an innate sin nature (Psalm 51:5; Romans 8:21)
- Blessings of Divine forgiveness bring freedom (Psalm 32:1-2, 5-6)
    - Our sins are covered
        - Freedom
        - Declared righteous
    - Iniquity is not imputed to us.
        - Clean slate
        - Full pardon
    - In us there is no deceit
        - Inward honesty
        - Honesty toward God
        - Honesty toward man
- A continuing need for forgiveness (1 John 1:6-9; Psalm 32:3-4)
    - Anguish when one does not seek forgiveness
        - The body worries
        - The body produces stress
        - The body holds anger
        - The body becomes bitter

- - The Lord is against those who do not seek forgiveness
    - The guilt cannot be hidden
    - We are separated from His protection
    - Our fellowship with God is disrupted
  - We have no strength when we keep our sins hidden
    - Strength is used keeping the secret
    - Can't use the strength of Jesus to ward off other sins

HUMAN FORGIVENESS (Matthew 6:12):
- We are to forgive as we have been forgiven
- Roadblocks to giving forgiveness:
  - The brother of the prodigal son shows three barriers (Luke 15:25-32)
    - Anger (v. 28)
    - Inability to see new truth (v. 29, 32)
    - Failure to be reconciled (v. 28)
  - The desire for vengeance hinders forgiveness (Romans 12:17-21, Leviticus 19:18)

Spiritual Anger Blocking Forgiving *(Adapted from Clinicians and Pastors Quick Reference Treatment Planner Software, AACC)*:

Which of these symptoms describe you, if any?
- ❏ Demanding from God
- ❏ Experiencing God as distant or punishing because your prayers or needs are not being met as you want
- ❏ Prideful and right in your eyesight
- ❏ Withdrawal from God due to feelings of rejection
- ❏ Frequent church changes or little fellowship
- ❏ Reject God's discipline as unwarranted
- ❏ Surrounds self with other angry or embittered Christians
- ❏ Little prayer or spiritual activity
- ❏ Avoids counsel from others
- ❏ A general mistrust of pastors, God, or fellow believers

"WHAT IS FORGIVENESS"[5]
(Carter and Minirth)

FORGIVENESS IS NOT:	FORGIVENESS IS:
• Letting go of healthy forms of anger	• Letting go of the demand for repayment
• Allowing others to continue to disrespect your needs and boundaries	• Freeing self to focus on rewarding relationships and pursuits.
• Lying down and becoming a human doormat	• Choosing to give-up obsessions regarding the wrongdoer.
• Telling the wrongdoer that the past is not longer significant and everything's fine now.	• Giving up resentment
• Agreeing to become best buddies with the wrongdoer.	• Willingly give up desire for revenge
• Pretending to go back to normal relations as if nothing happened.	• Giving up the ongoing temptation to insult the wrongdoer.
• Denying that you may still have to live with pain caused by the wrongful deed.	• Give up the illusions that you might have control over the wrongdoer's life.
	• Look forward to new opportunities that await you.
	• Give your permission to make life choices that will lead to contentment and peace.

---

[5] See Volume I, *Reflections on The Path to Wholeness, Journey of Faith,* for steps in seeking and giving forgiveness.

GROUP EXERCISE:
Philemon

Read Philemon 1-25:
- Describe the probable anger in Onesimus, Philemon
- Indicate the verses which describe the following forgiveness steps.
    - Admitting the hurt, attitude, feeling
    - Praying to see the person as God sees the person
    - Choosing to forgive
    - Forgiving
    - The Blessing
    - Prayer
- Type of Anger
    - Paul – Divine
    - Philemon – Righteous anger, material loss
    - Onesimus – None

Probable answers:
1. v 14
2. v 10 (a fellow prisoner, but a brother in Christ)
3. v 118
4. v 12
5. v 11
6. vv 23-25

Discuss other probable interpretations.

DROPPING THE ANGER

- A conscious decision
    - Recognize the anger
    - Define the anger
    - Describe why angry
    - Recognize you are loved
    - Recognize you can give love
    - Learn to be in control by making choices
    - Seek truth
    - Don't inflict anger on self
    - Use humility – show concern for others
    - Accept the limits of self and others
    - Identify fears
    - Build confidences
    - Nourish relationships

LISTENING DIFFUSES ANGER

Listening with Quickness (James 1:19-21):
- Listening results in doing righteously
  - The Greek – quick to listen is to listen without delay (no time lapse)
    - Immediate
    - Urgent
    - There is exercise of self-control of the tongue
    - Allows hearing God's Word
    - Allows teaching on the matter at hand
    - (Psalm 41:7) Listening will not "whisper against each other".
    - Listening protects against imagining bad/wrong things
    - (Proverbs 34:13) Listening will keep tongue from speaking lies
  - Slow to speak permits time to think on what heard
    - Appropriate responses
    - Use of wisdom in speaking
    - (Proverbs 31:17) Use of faithful instruction I responding
    - Listening builds/edifies (Proverb 11:13)
    - Listening does not destroy
  - Listening helps diffuse anger
    - Listening can lead to praise, not cursing (James 3:9-10)
    - Listening precedes fresh things (good things) coming out of mouth.

- Listening will show love, not anger (1 Corinthians 13:5)
    - (Proverbs 4:1,5) Listening opens one for instruction
        - Listening demands focus – paying attention
        - Listening required to gain understanding
        - Wisdom requires understanding

Argument for listening: - listening results in acting righteously:
"My dear brothers, take note of this: Everyo9ne should be quick to listen, slow to speak, and slow to become angry, for man's anger does not bring about the righteous life that God desires. Therefore, get rid of all moral fifth and the evil that is so prevalent and humbly accept the word planted in you, which can save you." (James 1:19-21)

Biblical Synonyms for the Verb – Listen
- To Hear
- To Obey
- To Publish
- To Discern
- To Reveal
- To Know

(Use a dictionary and concordance to see how used in various contexts)

BIBLICAL SITUATIONS OF LISTENING

SCRIPTURES	BIBLICAL LISTENING	CONTEXT
Genesis 3:8	Physiological Hearing	Garden of Eden, Adam and Eve heard the sound of God.
Numbers 9:8-9	Hearing to gain knowledge	Moses waits to hear from God regarding what to tell the Israelites as they prepare for the Passover.
Numbers 24:4	Spiritual and Physical hearing in agreement	Oracles, hearing and agreeing with the Word of God.
Numbers 22:21-22:36	Miracle hearing to gain attention	Balaam doesn't really hear the Angel of The Lord until the Lord get his attention through a speaking donkey.
1 Kings 3:9	Discernment in hearing	Solomon's request for a hearing heart to know right from wrong.
Matthew 6:7	Conciseness, sincerity & humbleness fosters being heard.	Do not think that a look of words will cause others to hear and to understand is Jesus' preface to the Model Prayer.
Luke 1:13	Divine Hearing	God answers prayers
Acts 16:25	Attentive Listening, sharing in oneness with someone else's prayer and psalm.	Prisoners shared the prayers & hymns of Ppaul and Silas and they shared in the response.
Acts 23:25	Judicious hearing as in court	The governor is to hear Paul's case.
2 Corinthians 6:1-2	Divine Hearing with Grace	God hears man's need and provided salvation.
James 1:19	Command to Listen with discernment and humility.	Avoid anger and unrighteousness.
James 1:22	Listen to act, obedience to what is heard	Avoid deceiving self and losing your blessing, act on what you hear from God
James 2:5	Command to Listen	Revelation from God, do not judge by the status of a person

LISTENING TO UNDERSTAND

- Paraphrase the content to ensure understanding.
- Paraphrase the feeling to ensure understand the hurt, irritations being expressed.

- Listening Carefully
    - Hear the feeling
    - Hear the emotion
    - Hear the verbal
    - Hear the non-verbal
    - Note any contradiction
    - Ask questions for clarification and to avoid misinterpretation

Role Play Quick Listening and Anger Control:
Son or daughter, delinquent from school, has joined a gang, is trying drugs, is HIV positive, is failing in school.
Mother/Father, single parent, normally works 7 days per week, often overtime, seeking to give child all the material comforts, and plans for future, does not kow friends, believes child is doing well in school. She/he home today and receives a call from school seeking a meeting to discuss issues. Other attempts, letters, calls, have never reached home.

Parent confronts the child.

- Use quick listening skills as much as possible
- Use anger control skills as much as possible.

Role Play Quick Listening with Discernment:
Speaker #1: Tell listener #1 four reasons why there should not be a separation of church and state.
Listener#1: Do not respond (verbally or non-verbally) to Speaker #1 until he/she is finished, and you tell Speaker #1 the content (not verbatim) and **meaning** of what Speaker #1 said.

Communication and Confrontation

Avoid the You Message:
- It is judgmental, evaluative, critical, blameful
- Doesn't normally contain information about your needs and feelings
- Diminishes the self-esteem of the other person
- Suggests the kind of change you feel should take place
- Tends to damage your relationship with the other person
- Creates feelings of defensiveness, aggression, withdrawal, denial, hurt, or resentment
- Assumes that guilt or fear will cause a change in behavior
- Samples:
    - You never even try to improve
    - Your problem is that you don't listen

- Use the I Message:
    - Includes active listening
    - Contains no direct suggestions or demands for how the other person must change
    - Helps the other person learn the effects of his/her behavior on others
    - Allows you to ventilate feelings while sharing your concern with the other person.
    - Samples
        - I am irritated when I am interrupted on the phone because I cannot listen to two conversations.
        - I get made when I am placed on hold because I normally have something else to do.
        - When papers are left all over the house, I am angry because I cannot find the sections I want to read.

- Keep the communication channels open (Baker, et al, Groups in Process).
- Identify your problems and desires
    - Am I the problem?
    - Is it my desires which are the stumbling block?
    - Have I adequately described my problem to self and others?
    - Have I clearly stated my desires?
    - Do I recognize that persons cannot respond to a disagreement, unless problem and desires clearly communicated?

SCRIPTURAL APPROACHES TO
PROBLEM-SOLVING

Mediation (Vine's):
I. N.T. – One who mediates between two parties with a view to produce peace.
II. One who seeks to establish a relationship between parties.

Argument: Mediation is an effective method of problem solving.
1 Timothy 2:5 (Amplified Version) There is only one God and [only] one Mediator between God and men, the *Man* Jesus Christ.
Romans 8:27 (NIV) And he who searches our hearts knows the mind of the Spirit, because the Spirit *intercedes* for the saints in accordance with God's Will.
Romans 34b: (NIV) Christ Jesus [Divine], …is at the right hand of God and is also interceding for us.

Argument: God permits different types of approaches to equitably solve problems.
Proverbs: 17:33 (NIV) The lot is cast into the lap, but its every decision is from the Lord.
Proverbs 16:22 (NIV) Plans fall for lack of counsel, but with many advisors they succeed.

MEDIATORS IN SCRIPTURES

SCRIPTURE	MEDIATOR	PARTIES IN DISPUTE	OUTCOME
1 Timothy 1:5	Christ Jesus	Sinners and God	Salvation & forgiveness
2 Corinthians 5:18	Christians	Non-believers and Christ	Reconciliation
Hebrew 8:6-7	Christ Jesus	Old Covenant of Law with Israel and God	New Covenant of promise and forgiveness
Galatians 3:19	Moses	Israel and The Law	Settlement of disputes
Exodus 18:17-23		Israel and God	Forgiveness
Judges 4:4-5	Prophetess Deborah	Israelites	Disputes were resolved.
1 Kings 3:16-28	King Solomon	Two mothers who had recently given birth	Wise ruling which reunited a real mother with her birth child.
Philemon 8-21	Paul	Onesimus and Philemon	Restoration of relationship as equals, equipped for service.

Examples of Problem Solving Techniques

APPROACH	OBJECTIVE	POSTURE	RATIONALE	LIKELY OUTCOME
FORCING **Scriptural Example** Ester 1:10-17	Get Your own way. Force Queen Vashti to exhibit herself before intoxicated nobles.	"I know what's right, don't question my judgment or authority." The King burned with anger, and advisors feared others would follow Vashti's example	It is better to risk causing a few hard feelings than to abandon an issue to which you are committed. Consulted experts in Matters of Law and justice and spoke to the wise men (1:13-14)	You feel vindicated, but the other party may feel defeated and possibly humiliated. King was vindicated by deposing the Queen, and to prevent other women from standing for dignity.
AVOIDING Scriptural Example **2 Samuel 13:1-38; 14:33**	Avoid having to deal with conflict David on hearing of his daughter's, Tamar's rape, took no action	"I am neutral on this issue; Let me think about it, That's someone else's problem" David did not attend the party of Absalom, and when Absalom killed Anon, David's son, the rapist, David took no action.	Disagreements are inherently bad because they create tension. David mourned Amnon's death, and longed for Absalom's return. Tamar had to live in Absalom's house.	Interpersonal problems don't get resolved causing long term frustration manifested in a variety of ways. Interpersonal problems existed between Absalom and David.
COMPROMISE **Scriptural Example** **Genesis 29:1-30; 30:25-31:1**	Reach an agreement quickly Jacob had to marry Leah, before he could marry the woman, Rachael, whom he loved.	"Let's find a solution we can each live with so we can get on with our lives" Jacob worked a 2nd seven years for Rachel.	Prolonged conflicts distract people from their work and engender bitter feelings. Jacob wanted to return to his home and Leban did not want him to leave. Jacob devised a plan to outwit Leban, transfer his wealth to Himself, and to return home.	Participants become conditioned to seek expedient rather than effective solutions. Jacob deceives Laban, flees to return home.

Examples of Problem Solving Techniques cont'd

APPROACH	OBJECTIVE	POSTURE	RATIONALE	LIKELY OUTCOME
ACCOMMODATING Scriptural Example: **Matthew 4:3-11**	Don't upset the other person Satan was seeking to entice Jesus to agree with him and to honor him.	"How can I get you to feel good about this encounter" Satan tries to tempt Jesus to depend on his divinity and relation to God and to depend on God for rescue.	A priority is to maintain a harmonious relationship. Satan tells Jesus, all this I will give you, if you bow down and worship me.	Other person is likely to take advantage. Satan was unsuccessful in getting Jesus to bow to Him where he would then be able to take His place.
COLLABORATING Scriptural Example: **Acts 15:1-29**	Solve the problem together Pharisees wanted new converts to become Jewish proselytes before they could become Christians. council meeting was called to discuss the issues.	"This is my problem, what is yours', I am committed to finding the best possible solution, What do the facts suggest. All groups came together, Apostles and elders and Peter, Church at Jerusalem, and Paul and Barnabus, Church at Antioch., relied on words of the prophets, actions of God and Holy spirit.	The position of all parties are equally important Let's not make it difficult for persons to turn to God.	The problem is most likely to be resolved. All parties are committed to the solution and satisfied that they have been treated fairly. Agreed that new converts did need to be circumcised, they would abstain from certain foods, and sexual immorality. The real issue was defined as faith and salvation.

SCRIPTURAL EXAMPLES OF PROBLEM SOLVING TECHNIQUES[6]

SCRIPTURE	PARTICIPANTS	PROCEDURES	OUTCOMES
Nehemiah 2:1-8	Nehemiah & King Artaxerxes	1. Defining the problem v 2-3 2. Prayer for guidance v 4a 3. Plan of action v 4b-8	Implementation of the solution.
Esther 4:4-8:17	Esther, King Xerxes, Mordecai, Haman	1. Investigation v4-8 2. Identification of obstacles v 9-11 3. Taking responsibility 12-15 4. Fasting [prayer?] v16 5. Developing an action plan 16c-17 6. Confronting the issue; implementing the plan.	Recognition for Mordecai, Victory for the Jews, death of the enemy, preservation of a people.
Daniel 1:1-16	Daniel, the guard, Hananiah, Mashael, Azariah.	1. Establish a goal v 8a 2. Confront the problem v8b-10 3. Take steps to implement solution 4. Test the solution v12-14 5. Confirm the action plan	Plan implemented with success, all parties satisfied.
Jonah 1:6-16	Jonah, Captain of the ship, sailors on board the ship.	1. Request for prayer v6 2. Cast lots (seeking God's answer) v7 for cause of problem 3. Investigate the cause v8-10 4. Find the best solution v12 5. Ask the Lord for guidance v14 6. Implement the solution	Problem of the storm solved.

---

[6] *Amplified Bible,* Zondervan, Ibid, *NIV.*

SCRIPTURE	PARTICIPANTS	PROCEDURES	OUTCOMES
Matthew 18:15-20 2 Corinthians 2:7-8	A believer who has sinned against a believer, and the believer sinned against	1. Confront the person of the fault v 15 2. If the person does not repent, take one or two witnesses and confront the person v 16 3. If the person does not repent, take the person before the church body. v17 4. If repentance is not complete exclude the person. 5. When the person repents bring the person back into the church.	Winning the believer, and loosing what has been loosed in Heaven and binding what has been bound in Heaven.
Romans 14:13-24	Immature believers and mature believers	1. Determine not to put a stumbling block in the path of the immature [mentorship] 2. Make every effort to achieve peace 3. Every effort to lift each other up v19 4. Abstain from any behavior which will further weaken the immature.v22	Strengthening the faith of the immature
1 Corinthians 1:10	Believers	1. Seek the Lord 2. Agree to come to an agreement 3. Agree to no divisions 4. Seek consensus in thought	Unity

I. Approaches to problem-solving in relational issues
    A. Help others increase sense of self-esteem using good will.
    B. Avoid giving directives
    C. Listen carefully
    D. Take all persons' concerns into account
    E. Ask questions so the other persons can examine his or her goals.

RULES FOR FAIR FIGHTING
(Adapted From Balswick and Balswick, The Family, 214-219)

1. Pray for Spiritual guidance, wisdom and patience.
2. Identify the issue(s).
3. Choose the right place.
4. Begin with a positive stroke.
5. Stick to the issue.
6. Do not bring up the past
7. Do not hit below the belt.
8. Take the other seriously.
9. Control any anger.
10. Express any anger non-abusively.
11. Do not play games.
12. Do not be passive aggressive.
13. Avoid asking for explanation of behavior.
14. Avoid labeling and name calling.
15. Avoid triangles
16. Remember God's love for all His creation.

BIBLIOGRAPHY

Biblical References

Barker, K. (Gen.Ed.)/ (1985) *The NIV Study Bible.* Grand Rapids, MI: Zondervan Bible Publishers.

Scofield, C.I., D.D. (1967) *The New Scofield Study Bible NKJV.* Nashville, TN: Thomas Nelson Publishers.

Thompson, F. C., (Ed.). (1993) *The Thompson Chain – Reference Bible, New American Standard.* Indianapolis, IN: B.B. Kirkbride Bible Co., 1993.

Lexicons/Dictionaries

Brown, F., Driver, S.R., & Briggs, C.A. (1930). *Hebrew and English Lexicon of the Old Testament.* Oxford: Clarendon Press, 1930.

Vine, W.E., Unger, Merrill F., White, William. *Vine's Complete Expository Dictionary of Old and New Testament Words.* Nashville: Thomas Nelson Publishers, 1985.

Organizational References

Training Manual for Developing Skills in Mediation and Peacemaking. Christian Conciliation Services, (1994, January).

Koehn Consulting. *Communication Skills For Managing Conflict..*

Books/Workbooks

Barker, L. et al. (1983). *Groups in Process.* (2nd ed.). Prentice-Hall

Barge, J. K., Managing Organizational Relationships. *Leadership Communication Skills for Organizations and Groups.* New York: St. Martin's Press, p. 142-172.

Carter, Ph.D., L. and Minirth, M.D., F. (1993). *Be Angry But Sin Not.* Nashville, TN: Thomas Nelson Publishers.

Carter, Ph.D., L. and Minirth, M.D., F. (1993). *The Anger Workbook.* Nashville, TN: Thomas Nelson Publishers.

Collins, G. (1995). *How to Be a People Helper.* (Rev. ed.). Wheaton, IL: Tyndale House Publisher.

Hemfelt, R. et al. (1991). *Love is a Choice: Recovery from Co-Dependent Relationships.* Nashville, TN: Thomas Nelson Publishers.

Sanke, Ken. *The Peacemaker. Grand Rapids, MI.* Baker BookHouse, 1991.

Whetton, D. A. & Cameron, K. S. (1991). *Developing Management Skills,* (2nd ed.). HarperCollins College Publishers.

Wilmot, W. W. & Hocker, J. (2001). *Interpersonal Conflict. 6th Ed.* Boston, MA: McGraw Hill.

Unpublished Works

Jackson, B. S. *A Correlational Analysis of The Relationship Between The Attitude of Trust Within A Communication Climate and Attitudes toward Union Among White-Collar Workers,* Unpublished Dissertation, Wayne State University, Michigan. 1981.

Jackson, B.S. *A Pilot Study: A Descriptive and Correlation Analysis of The Relationship Between Anger and Forgiveness.* Psychology 622, Michigan Theological Seminary, 2002.

Newspapers

David Briggs, Associated Press "Americans Discover Power of Forgiveness." p. 13A. The Detroit News. (December 21, 1997).

Chapter 4
LADY HAWK DOWN

Battlefield Blues – Women Under Attack

BSJ Christian Seminars
Minister Brenda Simuel Jackson, Ph.D.
© 2004 All rights reserved.

INCARCERATED IN THE MIND
©2008 Brenda Simuel Jackson

Incarcerated, separated by judgment from justice, and injustice alike.

Incarcerated, chased with thoughts of being molested, bullied, and having increased strife.

Incarcerated with thoughts that bind me to gloom.

Incarcerated, in my mind, stopping fruitful thoughts from bloom.

Release from these thoughts, a stronghold on my mind,

Peace, love and loosing, I seek to find.

Come MY Yoke is Easy, He said, and thoughts of Me will bring,

Beyond your mind, beyond your understanding, **divine, flowing, Springs.**

SEMINAR OBJECTIVES

- Recognizing psychological affliction
- Breaking mental strongholds
- Keeping hope alive
- Continuing your service to Christ and to others

Scriptures: 2 Corinthians 4:6-8; 6:3-10

Women Incarcerated (Analogy with Paul)

For God, who said, "Let light shine out of darkness, made His light shine in our heart to give us the light of knowledge of the glory of God in the Face of Christ...We are hard pressed on every side, but not crushed, perplexed, but not in despair; persecuted but not abandoned, struck down, but not destroyed. We always carry around in our body the death of Jesus, so that the life of Jesus may also be revealed in our body. For we who are alive are always being given over to death for Jesus' sake, so that His life may be revealed in our mortal bodies...

We put no stumbling block in anyone's path, so that our ministry [service], will not be discredited. Rather, as servants of God, we commend ourselves in every way: In great endurance, in troubles, in hardships, in distresses, in beatings, in imprisonment and riots, in hard work, in sleepless nights, and hunger, in purity, understanding, patience, and kindness, in the Holy Spirit and in the power of God; ;with weapons of righteousness in the right hand and in the left; through glory and dishonor, bad report and good report, genuine, yet regarded as impostors; known, yet regarded as unknown; dying, and yet we live on; beaten, and yet not killed; sorrowful, yet always rejoicing; poor yet making many rich; having nothing and yet possessing everything.

LADY HAWK DOWN

- The Hawk – Being Warlike
- On The Battlefield
- In the Armed Services of the Lord
- Shot Down

Definitions:

Ministering = Serving
- Διακονοσ – 2 Corinthian 3:6
- Servant of the Gospel
- Deaconess, Phoebe
- Servant of someone

Perplexed = Doubt (verb)
- Απορεω – be in great difficulty, doubt, embarrassment
- 2 Corinthian 1:8

Despair+ Perplexed[7]
- εξαπορεω – to be without a way
- Not having a way through

Persecuted = to be put to flight
- Διακω – to be pursued, where can one go?
- 2 Corinthian 4:9

---
[7] Play on words between perplexed and despair.

ATTACK SURVEY ASSESSMENT

How often do you feel the following attacks?
___ very seldom, ___ sometimes ___ often   ___ most of the time.

Check the one which best describes your attack(s)

HARD-PRESSED
___ very seldom   ___ sometimes ___ often   ___ most of the time

PERPLEXED:
___ Very seldom   ___ sometimes ___ often   ___ most of the time

PERSECUTED:
___ very seldom   ___ sometimes ___ often   ___ most of the time

STRUCK-DOWN:
___ very seldom   ___ sometimes ___ often   ___ most of the time

BATTLE LINES

<u>Spiritual</u>	<u>Mental/Emotional</u>
Drafted by God	Rejected by men and women in the body of Christ.
Enemy is Satan	Enemy is tradition
Enemy is Satan's Army	Enemy is resistance to change.
	Enemy is fear

PRISON VIOLENCE
(Attacks on the Mind)

- Dehumanization of being caged.
- Frustration of fear
- Lack of control of basic decisions
- On release, being labeled
- Carrying around silent rage
- Fighting an addiction
- Family rifts
- Wasting human talent
- Not using Spiritual gifts
- Waste of fiscal resources
- Unsure of achieving stability when released

BATTLE FATIGUE

- Feelings of Oppression/Depression/Stress
    - Dejected
    - Desperate
    - Discouraged
    - Hopeless
    - Pessimistic

- Color Me Blue
    - Low in Spirit
    - Puritanical
    - Profane
    - Indecent
    - Learned
    - Intellectual

Definition of Psychological Depression (Popular Definition – June Hunt)
- Involuntary reaction to situations
    - Rejection
    - Failure
    - Illness
    - Transitional stages in life (midlife crisis)
- Mind: Self doubt, worry, fear, forgetfulness
- Emotions: Anger, Sadness, Diminished joy
- Will: Irritability, activity pattern upset

Hidden Depression:
- Buried unresolved conflict
- Hurt is denied
- Buried in excessive activity
- The Mind: Self-inflation
    - Appearance of invincibility
    - Disorganized thoughts
- The Emotions: Suppressed anger
    - Distractions
    - Self-sacrifice
- The Will: Judgmentalism

Prolonged Depression
- Longer time needed for emotional recovery
- Interference with normal biological activities
- Interference with social activities
- The mind: Self criticism
    - Hypochondria
    - Inability to make decisions
- The Emotions: Anger
    - Hopelessness
    - No Pleasure
- The Will: Apathy
    - Diminished Activity

Major Depressive Disorder
- Loss of contact with reality
- Experiences of delusions, hallucinations

- The Mind: Self-rejection
    - Hallucinations
    - Lack of judgment or reasoning
- The Emotions: Acute Anger
    - Schizophrenia
    - No Pleasure
- The Will: Unresponsiveness - Catatonia

Biblical Descriptions of Oppression/Depression

- Distress (Isaiah 5:7)
- Injustice (Psalm 12:5)
- Extortion (Psalm 62:10; Jeremiah 22:17)
- Victimized (Leviticus 25:14)
- Feelings of being separated from God (Psalm 42:9) - "I say to God, my Rock, why have You forgotten me? Why must I go about mourning, oppressed by the enemy. My bones suffer mortal agony…saying to me all day long, where is your God?
- Feelings of hopelessness (Psalm 42:5, 11; 43:5) - Why are you downcast, O my soul? Why so disturbed within me? Put your hope I God, for I will yet praise Him, my Savior and my God.

THE MINDSET
- THE MIND

The Greek term for the mind, means the intellect in thought, feeling or will; the place of reflective consciousness, faculties of perception, and understanding, feeling, judging, and determining. It is often related to speaking.

KNOWING AND UNDERSTANDING:

DESCRIPTION	SCRIPTURE	REFERENCE	CONTEXT
Faculty to know	Luke 24:45	He opened their minds to understand the scripture	Jesus speaking to the disciples
Faculty for wrong actions	Romans 1:28	The depraved mind	God's response to the unbeliever
Faculty to be convicted, to be persuaded	Romans 14:5	Those weak in the faith	Paul describing to believers the effect of their actions on those weak in the faith
Faculty to pray and praise	1 Corinthians 14:15	Fruitful prayer	Paul explains to the Corinthians the role of the mind in fruitful prayer
Faculty to be vain (fruitless in thought)	Ephesians 4:17	Ignorance of Christ	Paul describing Ephesians who walk (live) according to their own thinking
Faculty to be protected	Philippians 4:7	Living the Christian Life	The peace of God protects the mind, emotions and thoughts.

REASONS WHY THE MIND IS THE BATTLEFIELD

DESCRIPTION	SCRIPTURE	REFERENCE	CONTEXT
Change is through the mind.	Romans 12:2	Transformation is through the mind.	Revealing God's righteousness through lifestyle.
Testing the will of God.	Romans 12:2	Knowing and enjoying the will of God.	The transformed life.
Spiritual renewal is in the mind.	Ephesians 4:23-24	A new Attitude	Living in the likeness of God.
Perception and Intent	1 Peter 4:1	Having the same attitude as Christ	Remain fervent in your love for Christ during the rough times (Peter is speaking)

THE BATTLE

We are destroying speculations and every lofty thing raised up against the knowledge of God, and we are taking every thought captive to the obedience of Christ. (NAU)

Romans 7:23:

But I see a different law in the members of my body, waging war against the law of my mind and making me a prisoner of the law of sin which is in my members. (NAU)

2 Corinthians 10:4

For the weapons of our warfare are not of the flesh, but divinely powerful for the destruction of fortresses.

THE OPPONENT

Satan uses false teachings, personal influence, impressive credentials, ande impressive speaking, and situations to impress the mind. (1 Corinthians 1:26) If we are going to fight the good fight, we need to know the opponent.

Satan/Mental Strongholds:

Character	Scripture	Action
The Tempter	Matthew 4:1-11	Tries t tempt Jesus
The Deceiver	Revelation 12:9	The Serpent in the garden of Eden who deceived Eve, the deceiver of the world
The Destroyer	Revelation 9:11	Destroyer of people in the Great tribulation
The Adversary	1 Peter 5:6	During times of suffering he seeks to devour
Controller of World Philosophy	2 Corinthians 4:7	Blinds the mind of the unbeliever
Defeated ruler of this world system	John 12:31	The world judged, and sin and death defeated
Controls the weak and shallow of faith	Ephesians 2:2	Causing the world not to take root, and shallow believers revert back to old way of life
Liar	John 8:44	Seeks to destroy the truth, freedom is through truth
Accuser	Revelations 12:	Accuses the believer before God.
Angel of light	2 Corinthians 11:15	Disguises himself so as to teach false doctrine and deceive the people.

WEAPONS OF THE ENEMY:
- Mindsets of Thoughts
    - A Stronghold – Ammunition
        - Built by ideas
        - Built through faulty reasoning
        - Built by faulty images of God
        - Built by blocking Truth
    - Place of bondage caused by certain ways of thinking
        - Planted through experiences in our lives

- Planted through faulty perceptions
- Planted through failure to examine self
  - Selfish Pride
  - Ego
  - Shame
  - Sin

TAKING THE OFFENSE
- Strategies for Victory
  - Identify the strongholds
  - Change how we think – Romans 12:2
  - Change how we reason[8]
- Know you are in a Battle
  - Check your self-conversation (Hunt)
    - __ I can't do anything right!
    - __ Why try?
    - __ My usefulness is over!
    - __ Look at so and so (by comparison)
    - __ I must have done something wrong
    - __ Nobody loves me.

    __ How many did you check?
  - The Light of the Truth:

The Lord says, I have loved you with an everlasting love, I have drawn you with loving-kindness. (Jeremiah 31:3)

---

[8] Romans 12:1 says spiritual service, this includes spiritual thinking.)

- What do you say about your situation?
  - __ I don't see anyway out!
  - __ It didn't matter anyway!
  - __ I can't do anything about it.!
  - __ I can't bear it!
  - __ This is intolerable!
  - __ It is not fair.
  - __ I am helpless to change the circumstances!

__ How many did you check?

- What is the light of the truth of this matter?

We can say with Paul, I can do everything through Him who gives me strength. (Philippians 4:13)

- What do you say about your future? (Hunt)
  - __ So What!
  - __ Nothing will change.
  - __ Its hopeless
  - __ I will be too old
  - __ That was my last chance.
  - __ I have nothing to live for!

__ How many did you check?

What is the light of truth

The Lord says, "For I know the plans I have for you, declares the Lord, plans to prosper you and to harm you, plans to give you hope and a future. (Jeremiah 29:11)

CHOOSING YOUR WEAPONS:

- The Word of God (John 8:31,32)
    - Truth over lies (Luke 4:1-13)
    - Follow Jesus' example – defeat of Satan in wilderness
    - "2 Samuel 22:29: You are my lamp, O Lord; the Lord turns my darkness into light."
    - Light in Dark Places

DARK THOUGHTS	SCRIPTURE LIGHT
I cannot escape this darkness	My God turns my darkness into light (Psalm 18:28)
I feel like I have no security.	Keep me safe, O God, for in you I take refuge. (Psalm 16:1)
I feel like I'm in much too much trouble!	God is our refuge and strength, an ever present help in trouble (Psalm 46:1)
I can't see the path I should take.	Trust in the Lord with all your heart and lean not on your own understanding; in all your ways acknowledge Him, and He will make your paths straight. (Proverbs 3:5-6)

- Missiles against Fear
    - __ 2 Timothy 1:7
    - __ Psalm 23:4
- Exercise Your Faith – Take on the Mind of Christ
- The faculty of retaining the knowledge given by God. (Romans 2:28)
    - Provides understanding of His call on your life.
    - Provides understanding of God's judgment.
    - Provides a consciousness of godly counsel.
    - Causes the Thinker to do what ought to be done.

- Reminds us of what Christ has done.
  - His life
  - His sign and wonders
  - His death on the cross
  - His burial
  - His resurrection
  - His appearances after the resurrection
  - His ascension
  - His sending the Holy Spirit
  - His mediation for us.
- Capture Any Reprobation:
  - Reprobate mind is opposite the Mind of Christ
    - Thinking rejected by God.
    - Flunked God's tests.
    - Refused to do what know to be based on knowing God.
    - Reprobate says one's faith is perverted, not the genuine thing.
- Mind of Christ guards against futile thinking. (Ephesians 4:17-19)
  - Guards against lack of godly knowledge.
  - Guards against hardening of the heart.
  - Guards against loss of sensitivity

You will remain unfit for duty if you do not forgive:
- Use the weapon of forgiveness
- Christ chose to forgive (Luke 23:24)
- Forgiveness starts in the mind.

SECRET WEAPONS – HOPE AND PRAISE

What is Hope?	What do we hope for?	What is the Impact of Hope
Reliance on the Lord (Psalm 39:7,31,23,24; 130:5-8)	Personal transformation and resurrection. (Acts 2:26;24:15; Romans 8:20-24)	Know there is a future. (Psalm 31:23,24)
Hope is Trust (Romans 15:13; 1 Peter 1:13)	A new Spiritual Life now. (Romans 8:9-11; Galatians 5:5; Ephesians 1:18-23)	Comfort (Psalm 119:49,50)
Hope says there is future.(Romans 8:24-25)	Success in trials (1 Peter 1:3-9)	Changed lives as we live as Christ taught and are led by the Holy Spirit (John 3:3)
Hope is Jesus Christ (Colossians 1:27)		Joy (Romans 5:2) Honesty with self (2 Corinthians 3:12), Positive Attitudes (1 Thessalonians 1:3; 1 Peter 3:15)

Praise, a ground to air missile:

- 1 Chronicle 16:25a: for great is the Lord and greatly to be praised:
    - Praise a response to God.
        - Reflect on what God has revealed about Hi8mself to us.
        - Deepen our sense of what God means to us.
        - Expresses God's goodness toward us.

GUIDED MISSLE OF PRAYER:

- Acknowledge God's existence (Matthew 6:9)
- Know that God knows and cares about us. (1 Peter 5:7; Matthew 6:31-34)
- Expect God is able and willing to respond. (James 1:5-8; 1John 5:14; Hebrew 4:16)
- Pray in the will of God. (1 John 5:14; James 4:14-15)

PREPARATION OF RETURN TO DUTY

- Pray
    - Deliverance
    - Recommitment
    - Praise
    - Petition
- Right Thinking
    - Line up thinking with the teaching of Christ (John 8:31-32)
    - Keep hope and Courage (Psalm 42:5)
    - Don't give up (Galatians 6:9; Isaiah 43:2)
    - Be Patient (Isaiah 40:31)
    - Trust in the Lord (Proverbs 3:5-6)
    - Depend on the Holy Spirit (1 Corinthians 2:10-16)
    - Put a watch on what you say, choose words carefully, a right mind and mouth go together (1 Peter 3:10)

THE LOGIC OF BIBLICAL "FOOLS"
BY
Minister Dr. Brenda S. Jackson, Ph.D.

Introduction

As I think over my life, I can remember when I thought and acted as a biblical fool (one without the knowledge of God as in Matthew 5:22). I acted as if I had no knowledge of God, as if my thoughts were all against the mind of the life giver, Jesus, The Christ. Although saved by faith in Jesus Christ, my thinking was as a fool void of God's wisdom. Although I was not given a Spirit of fear, I did not use the Spirit of power, love, and sound judgment. A fool's mind is like a fortress against thinking with the mind of Christ, thinking in thoughts of fear. Often this thinking is diagnosed as situational paranoia, panic distress, a phobia, or mental depression. The cure for such thinking included changing my thoughts.

Prolonged thinking as a fool will result in behavior which is contrary to living by faith. This thinking is built by allowing thoughts not of the Lord to control and to become strongholds in our minds. 2 Corinthians 10:3-6, explains how to overcome thinking like a "Fool". The theme is that fortresses of the mind are made of stones (thoughts) from the world, only Jesus can tear down the walls.

Fortresses in our mind:

A stronghold is a fortification, a fortress, sometimes built on a hill or some type of craggy rock which will make it difficult to capture. Cities such as Jericho, the earliest known stronghold, dated 7,000 B.C. and Jerusalem were fortified cities. How were these cities fortified? Walls were built around the city. These walls were built on stone foundations which were beneath the ground. The walls were made of stone. By Solomon's times, the fortification was a casement: two parallel stone walls with dividing partitions connecting them. The gates were chambered gates, like large rooms connecting the walls. During times of battle, the offender would lay a seige around the fortification, stop the flow of food and water to starve the inhabitants out of the fortress, and use battering rams to knock down the gates. From the wall the defender could see the enemy approaching and could throw stones and other defensive weapons down on the offender.

Today's fortification include intricate electronic systems which set off warnings when an offender breaches the set parameters, or there are mine fields of explosives. The attacker must find a way to get under the surveillance system or find a path way through the mine field.

Paul says our minds are like these fortresses, we have ideas, faulty reasonings, and false images of God which keep the truth from guiding us in our lives. We must find a way to batter down the gates, get under the surveillance, and to detect any mines which stop the truth from getting to the minds.

2 Corinthians 10:3-6:
2Cor 10:3 (NASB) For though we walk in the flesh, we do not war according to the flesh,
4 for the weapons of our warfare are not of the flesh, but divinely powerful for the destruction of fortresses.
5 [We are] destroying speculations and every lofty thing raised up against the knowledge of God, and [we are] taking every thought captive to the obedience of Christ,
6 and we are ready to punish all disobedience, whenever your obedience is complete.

Destroying the logic, walls, of the fortress:

The weapons needed to break down these walls are not of man but of God. As witnesses of God, our weapons are in the word of truth, in the power of God; by the weapons of righteousness for the right and the left. (2 Cor 6:7)

Our reasoning is through the word of God and not the word of man. Our goal is transformation of the minds of those who seek freedom. Romans 12:2-3 says, "And do not be conformed to this world but be transformed by the renewing of your mind,...For through the grace given...[do not]

think more highly of himself than he ought to think, but to think so as to have sound judgment, as God has allotted to each a measure of faith."

What are the stones of this mental wall made of? In Paul's day it was being gullible to eloquence of the smooth talker and that of human wisdom, walking by sight rather than by faith. (1 Corinthian 2 and 1 Corinthians 12-14) The pimp is a smooth talker; the politician is a smooth talker, showing the things of this world, and not the things of God.
There were false prophets to whom Paul was defending against, they were possibly claiming to be apostles and were promoting their own ideas, and attempting to discredit Paul and his message of Jesus Christ. Today, there are those who claim to have the word of God, but they deny the deity of Jesus Christ.

The biggest stone of the mind is self. Our own wisdom and thinking. Doing what is pleasing to the self and thinking of self strength rather than thinking on the power of Jesus Christ. Trying to reason without the wisdom, the experience, of God.

I have experienced those stone walls in the mind, and I ended with a diagnosis of paranoia. I knew that everyone was against me, and that someone was trying to kill me. It was only when I realized that Satan's battlefield is the mind, that I began to turn back to reality. My reality was in Jesus Christ and His strength. Thoughts of someone trying to kill me were replaced with who can be against me if God is for me!

What are the weapons to be used against such thinking? Rehabilitation won't bring down the wall of drugs, and metal detectors won't find all the mine fields which justify the prostitute being on the street. Our only weapon is Jesus Christ, and His Power. It was God's power that brought down the walls of Jericho and Jerusalem!
1 Corinthians 3:19-20:
Remember:

1Cor 3:19 (NASB) For the wisdom of this world is foolishness before God. For it is written, "[He is] the one who catches the wise in their craftiness";
20 and again, "The Lord knows the reasonings of the wise, that they are

useless."

 I guarantee you that man's wisdom is useless. My reasoning only kept me in the vicious cycle of paranoia, and looking over my shoulder, screening every call, cauling over every piece of mail, and being in constant worry and fear.

Thinking can only be changed when we belong to Christ and are obedient to Him. Breaking down fortresses of the mind, can only be done when we have the mind of Christ which comes through the knowledge gained from God's wisdom.

Let us destroy everything raised against the knowledge of God, with the only weapon assured of victory, Jesus.

BIBLIOGRAPHY

Bibles

Barker, K. (Gen.Ed.)/ (1985) *The NIV Study Bible.* Grand Rapids, MI: Zondervan Bible Publishers.

Thompson, F. C., (Ed.). (1993) *The Thompson Chain – Reference Bible, New American Standard.* Indianapolis, IN: B.B. Kirkbride Bible Co., 1993.

Books

Hunt, J. (2004). Depression, Walking from Darkness into Dawn. *Biblical Counseling Keys.* Dallas, TX: Hope for the Heart. p. 1-24.

Gengrich, F. Wilbur, D., Frederick W. (Eds.). (1979). *A Greek-English Lexicon of The New Testament and Other Early Christian Literature,* (2nd ed.). Chicago, IL: University of Chicago Press.

Johnson, E. L., & Jones, S. L. (2000). *Psychology & Christianity.* IL.: InterVarsity Press.

Meyer, J. (1995). *Battlefield of The Mind, Winning the Battle in Your Mind.* Tulsa, OK: Harrison House.

Chapter 5
REJECTION

BSJ Christian Seminars
Minister Brenda Simuel Jackson, Ph.D.
© 2006 All rights reserved.

STAMP OF REJECTION
© 2008 Brenda S. Jackson

Reject, that is who I am.

Reject, locked out like the water behind the dam.

Reject, there are none who care.

Reject, like I have a disease, none want to share.

Reject, should I have been born?

Reject, the one all scorn.

Reject? There is love in my future;

I've been grafted in by a Holy Divine Suture.

SEMINAR OBJECTIVES

- Understanding the Nature of Rejection
- Recognizing the Symptoms of feeling Rejection
- Recognizing how Feeling of Rejection affect Attitudes and Behaviors.
- Learning how to react Positively to Situations of Rejection

REJECTION

Scripture: Psalm 27:1-2, 7-10
Support Scriptures: Romans 8:27-29, 35-37
Theme: Confidence in The Lord overcomes all types of rejection.
- When rejected, we can feel confident.
- When rejected, we can act with confidence.
- When rejected, we have not fear of the outcome.

Background: Psalm 27 is a Psalm of David who is setting aside his fears of his enemies through his communion with God, and through his prayer (communication) with God. In Romans, Paul tells of righteousness, and warns against boasting of superiority between Gentile Christians and Jewish Christians, and Paul seeks to prevent a schism in the church.

The Word: Psalm 27:1-2 (NIV)
The Lord is my light and my salvation whom shall I fear?
The Lord is the stronghold of my life – of whom shall I be afraid?
When evil men advance against me to devour my flesh,
When my enemies and my foes attack me, they will stumble and fall.

27:7-10
Hear my voice when I call, O Lord; be merciful to me and answer me. My heart says of you, "Seek his face! Your face, Lord, I will seek. Do not hide your face from me, do not turn your servant away in anger; You have been my helper, Do not reject me or forsake me, O God my Savior.
Through my father and mother forsake me, the Lord will receive me

I. The meaning of being rejected

    A. **The Greek Term**

        1. To reject as in an exam

    2. To disallow

    3. Hebrew 12:17 – Esau rejected (disallowed from inheriting the blessing; he never repented selling his birth right.)

  B. The Greek Term

    1. To do away

    2. To Set aside

    3. To make void (refuse, or to break faith with as in Mark 6:26)

    4. To make void the counsel of God as in Luke 7:30

    5. To despise, to cast off as in 1 Timothy 5:12

  C. Hebrew Term

    1. Believers in a difficult situation may feel that God has turned against them

    2. To despise as an attitude

    3. Psalm 43: 1-2

Exposition:

I. v1 There is no fear when our confidence is in the Lord.

  A. God is Light.

    1. Light is our comfort.

    2. Light is our victory.

    3. Light is our hope.

  B. David was known as the Light of Israel.

    1. David was a conquer.

      a. David defeated Goliath

                b.   David's Servants (after he became King), defeated the Philistines.

                c.   The Brothers of Goliath were defeated. (2 Sam 21:15-22)

        2.   Yet David knew who was the true Light.

        3.   David knew where he got his help.

    C.   The Saving light was the Lord, that allowed David to prevail during his time of weakness.

II.   V 1b The Lord is my stronghold, my strength.

    A.   A stronghold is a fortress

        1.   Jericho walls were a stronghold built for protection.

        2.   Forts were strongholds for protection.

        3.   This prison is a fort.

        4.   Jericho walls came down with the strength of God.

        5.   The Lord's strength is everlasting, cannot be destroyed.

    B.   David proclaims the Lord's strength in his life, not that built by man.

    C.   The Lord is David's security fence.

    D.   Why did David rely on God's strength?

        1.   Past history, David had been victorious not because of his own strength.

        2.   David knew victory over his enemy, not by his strength, but the strength of The Lord.

        3.   We have overcome, but not by our might, but by His might.

III: v2 In times of adversities, like David we need to see past victories over our enemies.

    A. 2008, I am still here.

    B. 2007 is in the past!

IV. v 7. When David faced trouble, he went to seek the presence of The Lord.

    A. The fact that you can't get to Church, doesn't mean can't be in His presence.

    B. David couldn't get to the Tabernacle.

    C. Go to the Throne of Grace, Prayer Time.

        1. David knew he needed forgiveness for having doubted, and he sought God's mercy.

        2. Do not allow your attitude to stop you from getting into God's presence.

        3. Keep your confidence, that when you cry out, He will hear.

V. v9. Must pray as did David with your heart.

    A. Pray with total being.

        1. Pray with your physical being.

        2. Pray with your mental being.

        3. Pray with your emotional being.

    B. Seeking God's face is seeking His favor as well as His presence.

VI. V10: When I am as helpless as a poor orphan.

    A. If those who care are deceased.

    B. If those who care are showing tough love.

    C. Who cares? The Lord will take care – Faith!

- D. Derrick walked on Faith when he went to New Orleans, a place of desolation where people were leaving.

VII. VV 11-13 In the face of those who are lying about you.
- A. In the face of those who mean ill will.
  - When you feel rejected there is ambivalence in making decisions
  - When you feel rejected there is bitterness toward God and or the one who rejected you.
  - When you feel rejected there may be emotional withdrawal
  - When you feel rejected there may be the fear of being rejected again
  - When you feel rejected there may be guilt because of a relationship from which rejected
  - When you feel rejected you may be unable to accept love
  - When you feel rejected you may have an inability to trust
  - When you feel rejected you may become skeptical of the motives of others.
  - When you feel rejected you may make decision based on feelings instead of facts.
  - KEEP THE FAITH, OUR LORD DOES NOT REJECT:
- B. Lord, I keep faith, so show me the way, let me see your goodness again, now while I live.
  - Derrick (My biological son), saw goodness
  - Derrick got a ride.
  - Derrick got a job.

- Derrick got a place to stay.
- Goodness while he lives.

VIII. V14 – Wait on the Lord, be of good courage, know that deliverance is near.

Romans 8:27-29 (NKJV)
"We do not always know what to pray for or how best to pray, but we can know the purpose of God which the Holy Spirit desires to accomplish. The primary reference of all things is the suffering of this present time, all circumstances will work together in cooperation for the believer's good…the believer will be conformed to Jesus Christ now and reign with Him later."

Regardless of our situation, the Lord will not reject, The love of Christ for us never changes. His love for us cannot be broken, our security is unbroken.

I. Romans 8:37-8: No, in all these things we are more than conquerors through him who loved us. For I am convinced that neither angels, nor demons, neither the present nor the future, nor any powers, neither height nor depth, nor anything else in all creation, will be able to separate us from the love of God that is in Christ Jesus our Lord."
  A. Tribulations – The trials in life
  B. Distress, the suffering in life
  C. Persecution – Enemies seeking to keep us from reaching our goals.
  D. Famine – hunger
  E. Nakedness – being exposed
  F. Peril – The dangers in life
  G. Sword – Anger of those in authority
  H. Because of our faith, we are counted among those to be done away with
  I. Through all things, nothing will destroy the love between Christ and the true believers.
   - Neither fear of death or the hope of life

- Neither good angels, or bad demons
- Neither present troubles or fear of future troubles
- Neither prosperity or adversity
- Nothing created can separate the believer from the Love of He Who created all things.

II. Let us not reject ourselves because of past sins. (Colossians 1:21-22)
    A. Through Christ Jesus, we are Holy.
    B. Through Christ Jesus, we are blameless.
    C. Through Christ Jesus, we are beyond reproach.
    D. .You should feel deeply loved by God.
    E. You should feel completely forgiven by God.
    F. You should feel pleasing to God.
    G. You should feel accepted by God.
    H. Remember you are complete in Jesus Christ.

OVERCOMERS OF REJECTION

Scriptures	The Rejected	Overcoming Rejection	Applications
Acts 9:15-16 Acts 9:6-30 Acts 11:19-30	Paul (Saul) rejected by the disciples who were afraid of him because of his pre-conversion life of persecuting believers. Hellenists tried to Paul.	• Barnabus testified in behalf of Paul • Paul spoke boldly in the Name of Jesus • Paul went to Antioch preaching and teaching The Lord • Paul was used to take relief to Judea in time of famine • Paul chosen as an Apostle to the Gentiles	Paul kept his faith. Paul did not let rejection stop him from acting on his faith. Paul's rejection was used to benefit others, the Gentiles.
Genesis 37:1-50 Genesis 39:2-5 Genesis 50:19-20	Joseph rejected by his brothers because he was favored by his father, and because the Lord had shown his future as being in charge. They initially plotted to kill him, but ended in selling him into slavery.	• Depended on God, he did his job successfully • He was shown favor • Joseph was exalted to a position of power	He retained his faith, and over time (14 years) was rewarded. Through him the Lord preserved his people.

FEAR OF REJECTION[9]

Always	**Often**	**Sometimes**	**Seldom**	**Never**
1	2	3	4	5

___ 1. When I sense that someone might reject me, I become anxious.

___ 2. I spend lots of time analyzing why someone ignored me.

___ 3. It bothers me when someone is unfriendly to me.

___ 4. I am critical of others.

___ 5. I am shy and unsocial.

___ 6. I find myself trying to impress others.

___ 7. I become depressed when someone criticizes me.

___ 8. I always try to determine what people think of me.

---

[9] MCGEE. Robert S. *Search For Significance*, Rapha Publishing, 1993.

RESULTS OF REJECTION

Check the results of rejection that you have experienced.

___ Inability to give love.
___ Inability to receive love.
___ Avoiding people.
___ Being susceptible to experimenting with drugs.
___ Being susceptible to experimenting with sex.
___ Being susceptible to being manipulated
___ Anger
___ Resentment
___ Hostility
___ Depression
___ Defensiveness
___ Passive
___ Unwilling to share our faith

OVERCOMING THE ATTITUDE OF BEING REJECTED

- Admit the feeling (Lamentations 3:19-23)

- Claim God's acceptance and Unconditional Love. (Isaiah 54:10)

- Choose to Forgive those who rejected you. (Colossians 3:13)

- Draw on the power of scripture to see things through scriptural eyes. (Romans 12:2)

- Thank God for what you learned through the rejection. (Psalm 119:71)

- Draw on the power of Christ.

BIBLIOGRAPHY

Harris, S. L. (2006).*Understanding The Bible*. (7th ed.)/ Boston, MA: McGraw Hill.

McGee, R. S. (1993). *Search For Significance.* Nashville, TN: LifeWay Press.

Richards, L.O. *The Bible Reader's Companion.* Owings, MD: Offenheimer Publishers, Inc., 1991.

Walvoord, J.F. & Zuck, R. B. Eds. *The Bible Knowledge Commentary, New Testament.* Chariot Victor Publishing.

Chapter 6
SELECTING THE EASY YOKE

Breaking Yokes

BSJ Christian Seminars
Minister Brenda Simuel Jackson, Ph.D.
© 2005 All rights reserved.

YOKES
©2008 Brenda Simuel Jackson

Some yokes are made of steel, one was put on my wrists,

Because my conviction was real.

Another yoke hooked me to one, I did not need by my side.

A partner in deceit and deception, which created a life of lies.

I picked up another yoke, thinking it would set me free,

But my body and mind became bound as though tied to a tree.

Then, I picked up a yoke from a Man, Jesus, it fit, and was light as a breeze,

This yoke kept me on the right path, walking with ease.

SEMINAR OBJECTIVES

- Identify what are the various types of yokes.
    - Yokes that burden
    - Yokes that set free
- Identify means of breaking physical yokes through living in self-control of the Spirit.
- Establish goals to remain free from yokes that burden

FOUNDATIONAL SCRIPTURES

- Matthew 11:28-29 (Amplified Version)

Come to Me, all you who labor and are heavy laden and *overburdened,* and I will cause you to rest. [I will ease and relieve and refresh your souls.] Take my yoke upon you and learn of Me, for I am gentle (meek) and humble (lowly) in heart, and you will find (relief and ease and refreshment and recreation and blessed quiet for your souls. [Jeremiah 6:16]

- Matthew 11:30 (Amplified Version)

For My yoke is Wholesome (useful, good – not harsh, hard, sharp or pressing, but comfortable, gracious, and pleasant), and My burden is light and easy to be borne.

- Galatians 5:1 (Amplified Version)

In [this] freedom Christ has made us free [and completely liberated us]; stand fast then, and do not be hampered and held ensnared and submit again to a yoke of slavery [which you have once put off].

- Galatians 5:25 (Amplified Version)

If we live by the [Holy] Spirit, let us also walk by the Spirit. [If by the Holy Spirit we have our life in God, let us go forward walking in line, our conduct controlled by the Spirit.

A Yoke Is What?

- Generic – Denotative
    - Wooden bar to join two at the head or neck to enable working together
    - A device laid on the neck of a defeated person.
    - A device fitted to a person's shoulder t carry a heavy burden
    - An oppressive agency
        - Servitude
        - Bondage
        - Tie
        - Link
- Biblical Overview
    - Old Testament – imposed on the neck
        - A pole
        - A Band
        - Isaiah 10:27: A burden to be broken by the strong and sturdy.
        - As Israel grew strong, broke the hold of millions.
        - 1 Kings 12:4: Heavy labor without consent, forced labor.
        - Labor of Israelites under Solomon and Rehoboam.
    - New Testament – Greek term means to join
        - Verb
            - To put to work
            - To be linked
            - To be obligated

Sampling of Yokes of Destructive Habits

- Yokes which burden a person, physically, Spiritually, Mentally
    - Cheating
    - Compulsive gambling
    - Gossip/Slander

- Immorality
- Lying
- Pornography
- Profanity
- Sexual perversion
- Rage
- Sexual addiction
- Stealing
- Substance Abuse
- Violence
- Worry
- Yokes that Oppress
  - Lamentation 1:14
  - Sins will press down and sap your strength
- Yokes of Unnatural service
  - Leviticus 26:13
  - Yoke of involuntary slaves, being bowed down as was Israel under Egypt.
- Positive Yokes
  - Yoke of submission to Spiritual Authority
  - Matthew 11:29,30
  - Galatians 5:1

FOUR YOKES OF ABOMINATION
(Yokes learning to break in this Seminar)

- Lying
- Stealing
- Excessive Drinking
- Worrying

THE HABITUAL LIAR: The Deceiver

- To Beguile[10] – Old Testament meaning
  - Deal treacherously
  - In Aramaic, be sluggish
    - Be putrid
    - Be corrupt
  - Deceive
  - Mislead
- The Craft of Deception – Old Testament Meaning:
  - To deceive as a craft such as fraud.
  - Deceit of balances is called craftiness.
- Another root term is translated as lying means to cheat.
  - To be untrue
- The Falsehood
  - Opposite of falsehood is <u>faithfulness:</u>
    - Falsehood – inability to keep faith
    - Vain words (Exodus 5:9) are lies
    - Deceptive speech
  - Greek pseudo meaning fictitious[11]
    - Describes hypocritical liars
    - Deceptive spirits (demons)
  - Idolatry
    - A lie – an idol worshipped in lieu of God (Romans 1:25)
    - The lie, a man made idol (Isaiah 44:20)
  - Pathological Lying ("Counseling Through The Bible, June Hunt, p. 3)
    - Compulsive Lying
    - Vague
    - Seemingly Purposeless

---

[10] When used to mean deceit or treachery, often refers to spoken speech.
[11] English tern is pseudonymn.

- May believe the Lies
- May have no discernible guilt

IN THE BEGINNING THERE WAS DECEPTION

Scriptures	Deceit	Context	Outcome/injuries
Genesis 3:1-4	Satan deceives Eve	Satan seeking to displace God	Fall of man, beginning of original sin.
Genesis 20:1-4	Abraham deceives Abimelech saying Sarah is his sister[12]	Abraham seeks to protect himself from one with ore power[13]	Abimelech took Sarah and The Lord was on the verge of destroying a nation.
Genesis 27:5	Rebekah and Jacob deceive Isaac	Isaach believes he is dying and as custom, he is giving the blessing to the eldest son which is not Jacob.	Jacob gets Isaac's blessing, and then must flee to avoid the wrath of Esau, the family is split. Sarah never saw her son again.
Genesis 29:15-27	Leban deceives Jacob giving him Leah as wife and not his love.	Jacob Hs requested Rebekah, worked seven years for her dowry to have her as wife, but she was the youngest, and Leah the oldest.	Beginning of a rif between Jacob and Leban, and Jacob had two wives, and not only the one he truly loved.
Genesis 39:7-21	Joseph is imprisoned because he refused the advances of Potiphar's wife.	The wife was pursuing Joseph a servant and he refused to violate his master's trust, and she lied against him, and accused him of molesting her.	Joseph, innocent, imprisoned for two years

---

[12] Sarah is Abraham's half sister.
[13] Abraham lied twice to gain personal protection, showing a lack of trust in God, and putting his wife at risk.

MY PERSONAL EXAMINATION

My Deception	The Context	The Outcome

GOD'S COMMANDS

Colossians 3:9-10

- Do not lie to each other since you have taken off your old self with its practices, and have put on the new self, which is being renewed in knowledge in the image of its creator.
- Ephesians 4:25

Therefore each of you must put off falsehood and speak truthfully to his neighbor, for we are all lmembers of one body.

Anatomy of the Falsehood

- F – Fallacies against The Logos, Poor Logic
- A- Anti-Christ, going ainst the truth of God
- L – Lies accepted in lieu of the Truth of God
- S – Self-centered, and not Christ-centered
- E – Evilness over righteousness
- H – Honor of thievery
- O – Odor of deception
- O – Oneness with demons
- D – Deceit is your god (Idol)
- Richards says: "There is a call to live with each other honestly sharing realities rather than attempting to project illusions that made us appear better than we are. The portrait of falsehood and deceit suggested by the Hebraic word is far from pretty. Actions are words designed to deceive are not supported by reality, worse they violate the basic relationships of trust and honesty that are to exist between human beings."

Breaking the Yoke of Lying and Putting on the Yoke of Truth

- Know you are not accountable for how others respond to the truth (1 timothy 2:25-26)
- Know the consequences of deceit. (Psalm 5:6)
- Examine Your motives (Psalm 51:6)

- Determine to be honest with God. (Psalm 32)
- Depend on the Strength of Christ to enable your change. (Philippians 4:13)
- Know God's Word about lying and deceitfulness.
- Pray
    - Discern truth from lies
    - Conviction in all deceit
    - Know the full consequences of any manner of deceit.
    - Boldness to speak truth factually, and with love.
- Treat Truth as a Valued Treasure (Counseling through The Bible, Ibid)
    - Consciously choose truth over a lie
    - Check your life style to see how it measures sto God's truth scale
    - Always report the full truth with all facts
    - Reverence Truth
    - Ask Yourself:
        - Did I speak truth?Did I act truthfully?
        - Did I Omit truth? Were my motives righteous?

PERSONAL INVENTORY

Identify and examine lies told/telling although did not think of them as lies initially. Journal the results.

___ I have no money.

___ I have a conflict and I cannot attend.

___ I feel good.

___ I quit smoking without a struggle.

___ I don't steal.

___ I always seek the good of the other person.

___ I always seek the truth.

II. STEALING
God's Commands Regarding "Stealing":
- Exodus 20:15 – You shall not steal
- Leviticus 19:11 – "...I am the Lord your God. Do not steal, do not lie. Do not deceive one another. Do not swear falsely by my name, and so profane the name of your God...Do not defraud your neighbor or rob him. Do not hold back the wages of a hired man overnight.
- Matthew 19:18: "... do not steal...

Anatomy of Stealing

- Act of stealing is same as lying.
    - As an adjective: Act of cover-up
        - 2 Samuel 19:3, The men **stole** into the city that day as men **steal** in who are ashamed when they flee from battle
        - Cowards
    - As verb: To steal by implication is to deceive.
    - As a righteous motive:
        - Proverbs 6:30-31- "Men do not despise a thief if he steals to satisfy his hunger when he is *starving*. Yet if he is *caught, he must pay sevenfold*, though it cost him all the wealth of his house.
    - Legal Fraud, Luke 19:8:
        - In the collection of taxes fraudulently [with government sanction], overcharging.
        - "Zacchaeus as chief publican admitted possible fraud, but agreed to restore fourfold, if found. (Customs and Manners, p. 178.)

Denotative Meaning of Stealing (Webster)

- Taking without right of permission that which belongs to another.
- Keeping others from receiving what is their right.
- Synonyms for stealing (New World Thesaurus)
    - Filch
    - Loot
    - Rob

- Purloin
- Embezzle
- Defraud
- Appropriate
- Abduct
- Strip
- Poach
- Swindle
- Plagiarize
- Blackmail
- Shoplift
- Fleece
- Plunder
- Slander
- Extort
- Kleptomania[14] (Webster's Dictionary)
- Copyright infringement

---

[14] Persistent neurotic impulseto steal, without economic motive, only an emotional reward,.

Self Examination of Personal Theft

Stealing from God:
- I did not pay tithes and offering.
- I did not serve God with my talents.
- I have not served God with my time.

Stealing from an Office:
- I used supplies for personal use.
- I took a friend to lunch and charged it to business.
- I charged personal items to the company.
- I used company gas for personal use.
- I used the copier without paying for personal copies.
- I cam to work late, and/or left early.
- I called in sick when I was not sick.

Stealing from Businesses:
- I kept an overpayment.
- I falsified insurance claims.
- I violated copyright laws.
- I downloaded someone else's music without paying.

Stealing from relatives, Friends, Strangers:
- I have taken money.
- I Have borrowed items, and failed to return them.
- I have received monies fraudulently.
- I cheat at play.
- O live at home without paying rent or purchasing food, or paying toward utilities.
- I have stolen items, sold, or pawned them.
- I have found items with identification and failed to return them.

Stealing from Government:
- I claimed invalid deductions on my income taxes.
- I purchased personal items with a tax exempt number.
- I claimed charitable contributions not made.
- I did not pay duty on all items purchased outside of the country.

Others forms of stealing:
- I collected rent from property I did not own.
- I fraudulently hooked into someone else's utility(ies).
- I used someone else's identify to obtain credit, monies, service.

BREAKING THE YOKE OF STEALING

- Pray and ask God to re4veal to you the ways in which you steal, and have stolen.
- Confess the results to a person who will hold you accountable.
- Start a journal, and record all things stolen, and actions taken for restoration.
- Pray for God to reveal to you any false rationalizations (i.e. he.she owes me).
- Listen to the prompting of the Holy Spirit.
- Put on the Full Armor (Ephesians 6:13-18)
- Seek and accept forgiveness from God.
- Seek forgiveness of those sinned against.
- Seek to make restitution.
- Remember stealing is disobedient to God.
- Remember Stealing dishonors God. (Proverbs 30:9b)
- Tell yourself:
    - Stealing says I do not trust God. (Matthew 7:25-32)
    - Stealing puts priority on possessions for fulfillment.
    - Stealing says I am smarter than anyone else.
    - Stealing is a way of vengeance, God said Vengeance is His.
- Avoid being jealous.
- Avoid Envying.
- Remember Ephesians 4:28:
    - He who has been stealing must steal no longer, but must work doing somethi9ng useful with his own hands, that he may have something to share with those in need.
    - Seek to help not to harm.

Remember Philippians 4:19: "My God will meet all your needs according to his glorious riches in Christ Jesus.

ALCOHOL ABUSE and GETTING HIGH
(Being Drunk on fermented drink)
1 Thessalonians 5:6-11:

So then, let us not be like others, who are asleep, but let us be alert and self-controlled. For those who sleep, sleep at night, and those who get drunk, get drunk at night. But since we belong to the day, let us be self-controlled, putting on faith and love as a breastplate, and the hope of salvation as a helmet. For God did not appoint us to suffer wrath but to receive salvation through our Lord Jesus Christ. He died for us so that, whether we are awake or asleep, we may live together with Him. Therefore encourage one another and build each other up, just as in fact you are doing.

- It is getting drunk that puts us in darkness.
- Addiction:
    - Compulsive use of Substances
        - Drugs (Includes prescriptions)
        - Alcohol
        - Chocolate or other edibles
        - Carbonated drink such as Colas

Compulsive Drinking:

Biblical History – Strong Drink – Two types of Wine
- Unfermented wine (New Wine) associated with blessings
- Fermented Drink:
    - Feasts
    - Gifts
    - Special occasions
- Initially wine, beer, acceptable social drink.
- Fermentation, chemical change.
- The Last Supper:
    - Phase is "fruit of the Vine", Matthew 26:29. (NIV, NASB, The Greek New Testament)
        - May be fermented
        - May be unfermented

Drinking that is not of the Spirit:

Drink	Drunkenness
Ecclesiastes 10:17: Persons are blessed who drink not to get drunk.	Ephesians 5:18: Do not get drunk on wine, leads to debauchery (Greek term for orgies, wantonness, licentiousness.)
Deuteronomy 7:13: Unfermented wine is associated with a blessing as in produce/crop.	1 Corinthian 5:11: Do not associate with a Christian (brother or sister) who is a drunkard.

1 Samuel 25:18: Fermented wine given as a gift of reconciliation and sustenance.	Galatians 5:19,21: The acts of the sinful nature…envy, drunkenness, orgies.
Numbers 6:3: Strong drink is any fermented fruit or grain.	1 Corinthian 11:19-22: Getting drunk is humiliating and raising the question of despising the Church of God.
Diluted wine used in Passover (Customs and d Manners)	Proverbs 20:1: Drunkenness shows lack of wisdom.
Exodus 29:40: Drink Offering sacrificed to God has a pleasant aroma.	Proverbs 21:17b: lavish drinking will cause the loss of riches
Genesis 14:18: Drink is used for refreshment.	Habakkkuk 2:15: Drunkenness leads to immoral behavior, and anyone who causes such drinking will be judged.
2 Chronicle 11:11: Wine used in time of war to give soldiers strength in case of a siege.	2 Samuel 13:28: Will cause one not to be aware of the danger around them.
Deuteronomy 14:26: Wine or other fermented drink used to rejoice before the Lord.	Proverbs 31:4: Persons in authority are not to crave strong drink because their drinking may cause them to forget laws, and they may become oppressive.
	1 Peter 4:3: Non-Christian behavior includes drunkenness.
	Luke 21:34,36: The persons who are drunk when Christ returns will not be ready for His return (No blessings)

God Commands Self Control: (1 Thessalonians 5:6-8)
- o   Without self-control there is not godliness (2 Timothy 3:3)
    - o   Without self-control in the Greek is the same as being incontinent.
    - o   Without self-control in the Greek is being without power.
- o   Power is living by the Holy Spirit (Galatians 5:16)
    - o   So I say live by the Spirit, and you will not gratify the desires of the sinful nature.
- o   Living By The Spirit
    - o   Allow the Fruit of The Spirit to grow. (Galatians 5:22-23)

- - - Fruit starts to grow with the acceptance of Jesus Christ as Lord and Savior.
    - Fruit starts to grow with your faith, and rebirth.
  - Plant in you what will please the Spirit, and not flesh. (Galatians 6:8)
  - When under pressure do a work for the Lord. (Galatians 6:9)
  - Focus your mind on what the Spirit desires. (Romans 8:5)
  - Know, your body will suffer.
  - Know victory is in Christ. (Romans 8:17,18)
  - Seek not being a slave to your flesh.
  - Pray
  - Depend on The Holy Spirit to help during periods of weakness.
  - Know the Godhead is fighting your battle.
    - God is for you. (Romans 8:27)
    - The Holy Spirit is interceding for you. (Romans 8:31)
    - Jesus Christ is interceding for you. (Romans 8:34)

IV. BE ANXIOUS FOR NOTHING

My Anxious Thoughts:

Self Test:

- I am anxious about _____
- I am concerned about _____
- I am distracted by _____
- I am divided by _____
- I am weighed down thinking about _____

The Yoke of Worry:
- Psalms 139:23:
    - Search me, O God, and know my heart;
    - Test me and know my anxious thoughts.
- Unfruitfulness of worry – Luke 21:34
    - Weighs down the heart
    - Saps energy
    - Leads to drunkenness
    - Is like a trap
    - Worry causes the rejection of the Word of Life
        - Matthew 13:22, Mark 4:19; Luke 8:14

        The one who received the see that fell among the thorns is the man who hears the word, but the **worries** of this life and the deceitfulness of wealth choke it, making it unfruitful.

- The Greek term for worry often translated "cares" (KJV)
    - Concerned about the future
    - Anxious expectation (Encyclopedia of Bible Words, Richards)
- Healthy Concern – motivated about something which you have control
    - Increases Creativity
    - Promotes Initiative
    - Guides Focusing

- Directs the mind to the important
- Legitimate Worry:
    - Concern with the Lord's affairs.
    - How to please the Lord (1 Corinthians 7:32)
    - A married person has divided concerns:
        - How to please the wife/husband
        - How to please The Lord simultaneously
    - Members of the body of Christ have concern for each other (1 Corinthians 12:25-26)
    - Pastors are concerned for other churches (2 Corinthians 11:28)
- Unrighteous Worry (Matthew 6:25-34)
    - Worrying about the material things of life.
    - Not living by faith.
    - Worrying about things over which have no control.
    - Worrying about things which non-believers chase.
    - Worrying about tomorrow.
    - Worrying about how will defend yourself before non-believers (Luke 12:11-12)
- Misdirected Worry (Luke 41-42)
    - Worrying about good works rather than spending time with Jesus

    Martha was told by Jesus that she was upset over minor things, but Mary had chosen the better things.

Causes of Worry:
- Misplaced trust.
    - Trusting men whose hearts are no in the Lord.
    - Walking in the flesh.
    - Jeremiah 17:5: Cursed is the one who trusts in man, who depends on flesh for strength, whose heart turns away from the Lord.

Breaking The Yoke:
- Handling the Worry (1 Peter 5:6-9)

- Cast all your anxiety on Him, because He cares for you.
- How to Cast:
    - Bait is faith
    - Be humble to God.
    - Be self-controlled through the Holy Spirit.
    - Be alert – know the plows of Satan and the flesh
    - Know that others are in similar situations.
    - Depend on God.
- Pray (Philippians 4:6)
    - Ask for what is needed
    - Give Thanks
    - Bring peace to your hearts and minds
- Wait with patience
- Think truth
- Think on the good
    - Know patience comes through trials (James 1:3)
    - Be joyful in hope (Romans 12:12)

BIBLIOGRAPHY

Bibles

Amplified Bible. (1987). Grand Rapids, MI: Zondervan Bible Publishers.

Barker, K. (Gen Ed.), (1985) *The NIV Study Bible,* Grand Rapids, MI: Zondervan,

Books

Center for Substance Abuse Services. (1996). *Effective Substance Abuse Counseling With Specific Population Groups.* Michigan Department of Health.

Center for Substance Abuse Services. (1996). *Fundamentals of Alcohol and Other Drug Problems.* Michigan Department of Health.

Hunt, J. (2004). Catch the Thief Hiding in Your Heart. *Biblical Counseling Keys.* Dallas, TX: Hope for the Heart. p. 1-4.

Hunt, J. (2004). God's Word for Worried Hearts. *Biblical Counseling Keys.* Dallas, TX: Hope for the Heart.

Gingrich, F.W. and Danker, F. W. (1958). *A Greek-English Lexicon of the New Testament and Other Early Christian Literature.* Chicago, IL: University of Chicago Press.

Gower, R. (1987). *The New Manners and Customs of the Bible Times.* Chicago, IL: Moody Press.

Laird, C. (1974). *Webster's New World Thesaurus.* New York: Popular Library.

Webster's Seventh New Collegiate Dictionary. (1967). Springfield, MA: G & C Merriam Company Publishers.

Chapter 7
ENDURING THE TOUGH TIMES

Continuing in Spite of

BSJ Christian Seminars
Minister Brenda Simuel Jackson, Ph.D.
© 2005 All rights reserved.

GOING THROUGH
©2008 Brenda Simuel Jackson

Going through tough times lets one know living is not a cinch.

Tough times are used by God to teach His strength.

The reborn, divinely adopted have an endurance trait in their spiritual DNA.

Those going through outgrow fear and become bold in faith.

Those going through learn to pray, to break yokes, study God's Word and praise Him.

On the rough side of the mountain, those going over, climb knowing Jesus is the light, never growing dim.

To those going through, hoping in Christ Jesus continuing through, victory is guaranteed.

SEMINAR OBJECTIVES

- The participant will gain an understanding of what is suffering for benefit.
- The participant will learn what is suffering because of sin.
- The participant will learn how to handle affliction of any kind.
- The participant will understand endurance during trials

GUIDING SCRIPTURES

- 1 Peter 5:6-11
- James 1:2-7
- Hebrew 12:5-7

ENDURING THE TOUGH TIMES

Argument:
Although we are in Christ Jesus, we will have trials and suffer.

- We suffer because we are human and the body is decaying
- We suffer because of sin.
- We have trials to keep us from sinning.
- We have trials and we suffer to perfect our character.
- We suffer to share in the character of Christ.
- We have trials and suffer to teach us how to minister to others.

Scriptures: 1 Peter 5:6-10
- Humble yourselves, therefore, under the mighty hand of God, that He may exalt you at the proper time.
- Casting all your anxiety upon Him, because He cares for you.
- Be of sober [spirit], be on the alert. Your adversary, the devil, prowls about like a roaring lion, seeking someone to devour.
- But resist him, firm in [your] faith, knowing that the same experiences of suffering are being accomplished by your brethren who are in the world.
- And after you have suffered for a little while, the God of all grace, who called you to His eternal glory in Christ, will Himself perfect, confirm, strengthen [and] establish you. (NASB)

James 1: 2-7
- Consider it pure joy, my brothers, whenever you face trials of many kinds,
- Because you know that the testing of your faith develops perseverance.
- Perseverance must finish its work so that you may be mature and complete, not lacking anything.
- If any of you lacks wisdom, he should ask God, who gives generously to all without finding fault, and it will be given to him.
- But when he asks, he must ask and not doubt, because he who doubts is like a wave of the sea, blown and tossed by the wind.
- That man should not think he will receive anything from the Lord; he is a double-minded man, unstable in all he does. (NIV)

Hebrews 12: 5-7

- And you have forgotten that word of encouragement that addresses you as sons: My son, do not make light of the Lord's discipline, and do not lose heart when he rebukes you,
- Because the Lord disciplines those he loves, and he punishes everyone he accepts as a son,
- Endure hardship as discipline; God is treating you as sons. For what son is not disciplined by his father?

The Meaning of Suffering:
- To Be afflicted (2 Corinthians 1:4, 2:4; 4:17; 1:4,8)
- Distressed from an external source
- Mental state of Mind.
- Spiritual state of Mind.
- Dismay and Anguish (BDB)

The Meaning of Suffering:
"To undergo something painful or unpleasant, whether a physical injury, emotional pain, grief, or loss." (Richards, Lawrence. Bible Dictionary, 952)

The Meaning of "Trial":
- An attempt to prove the quality of someone or something
- The purification of Saints (Jeremiah 6:27-30)
- A difficult situation experienced by believers
- A legal proceeding to test one's guilt or innocence.

Endurance:
"For His anger lasts only a moment but His favor lasts a lifetime; weeping may endure (remain), for a night, but rejoicing comes in the morning. (Psalm 30:5)
- Endurance relates to results which are commendable.
- Endurance does not discredit.

Negative Endurance:
Before Prison, how did you endure?
- Followed the crowd?
- Ran away from home?
- Abandoned the church?
- Became drug dependent?
- Struck out at authorities?
- Dropped out of school?

ENDURANCE

Scripture	Definition	Biblical Context	Application
Genesis 33:14	To endure walking	Jacob is meeting Esau after a separation, and he seeks to lead at such as pace that the Children will be able to walk.	There is a need for physical endurance; how we walk in this life.
Exodus 18:23	To endure is to arise, to confirm, to continue to stand.	Moses is being counseled by his father-in law, regarding his need for assistance if he is to endure the strain.	Sometimes help is needed in order to Endure.
Psalm 30:5	To Endure is to stay	The temple is being dedicated to the Lord, and the worshippers feel security and seek to praise Him. Struggles are temporary in comparison to God's favor.	We need to stay in God's counsel during struggles, remember struggles are temporary, but God's favor is everlasting.
Matthew 10:22	To endure is to bear up courageously.	"All men will hate you because of me, but he who stands firm to the end will be saved". Jesus Counsels his disciples as He sends them forth.	We must remember that doing God's will does not always lead to smooth sailing. The world will continue to stand against you.
Matthew 24:33	To endure is to bear up under trials. It is to have fortitude.	"But he who stands firm to the end will be saved". Jesus encourages his followers.	To endure is to know that God shall rescuer.
Mark 4:11	To endure is to have firm roots.	"But since they have no root, they endure only a short time. When trouble or persecution comes because of the word, they quickly fall away.	Only true believers can endure for the Gospel.
John 6:27	To endure is to live for the Lord. To endure is to be in state of expectancy.	Do not work for food that spoils, but for food that endures to eternal life which the Son of man will give you. On Him God the Father has placed His seal of approval.	Endurance is not in reference to material things which are temporary, but for spiritual treasures that are forever. An example would be patience, a fruit of the Spirit.

Scriptures	Definition	Biblical Context	Application
2 Corinthians 1:6	Endurance is cheerful, patient continuance.	Paul is willing to be distressed to learn to give comfort, and encouragement to others. "We receive comfort and consolation because you are comforted".	Gain comfort from enduring distress, because we are learning how to help others.
Hebrew 11:27	To endure is to act in faith.	"By faith he left Egypt not fearing the King's anger; he persevered because he saw Him who is invisible. Moses led by faith.	Faith is needed to endure when the end is not known.
2 Timothy 2:3	To endure is to undergo hardships, to suffer trouble, to endure afflictions.	Paul is telling Timothy to endure the hardship like a good soldier of Christ Jesus.	The Believer seek to please the Commander in Chief, Jesus Christ.
Hebrew 6:15	To endure is to be long-spirited, patient.	The writer of Hebrews reminds us of Abraham's patience, "I will surely bless you and give you many descendants. And so after waiting patiently, Abraham received what was promised.	We must know that God's promises are true.
1 Peter 2:19	To endure is to bear up under unjust hardship	"For it is commendable if a man bears up under the pain of unjust suffering because he is conscious of God."	God looks with favor on those who suffer for Him. This gives peace.

Paul's Suffering:
- 2 Corinthians 6:3-10
    - Threatened by angry mobs
    - Beaten several times
    - Ship wrecked
    - Imprisoned on several occasions
    - In bonds seven times

Job's Suffering:
- Job 1:1 – 2:10
    - Loss of children
    - Loss of wealth
    - Loss of servants
    - Loss of Status
    - Loss of Health

Your Tough Times:
Description:

How did you endure?

How to endure:
- Receive encouragement from the suffering
- Have hope in Deliverance
- Maintain a Spiritual attitude
- Count trials as Joy.
- Receive God's comfort
- Encourage others

ENDURING SUFFERING THROUGH ENCOURAGEMENT

I. <u>Gaining strength, repairing one's emotions, and/or fortifying oneself to continue is encouragement.</u>

    A. Paul knew that encouragement had to match suffering if one was to gain strength (2nd Corinthians 1:3-7)

    B. The sources of encouragement are internal to self and from external sources.

        1. The Corinthians shared in suffering with the Apostles; through this sharing, they shared with each other in God's encouragement.

            a. Persons who have experienced the same suffering can encourage others who are going through the situation.

            b. Encouragement is through God's Word.

            c. Encouragement is through Faith of deliverance.

        2. Joshua was encouraged in his struggle because he knew the outcome.

            a. Deuteronomy 1:38: Because Joshua was obedient and believed, he was encouraged.

            b. "Joshua…will enter…encourage him because he will lead Israel to inherit it."

        3. The wicked encourage each other in their plans.

            a. They talk about their schemes.

            b. They believe each others' lies. (Ps. 64:5)

        4. 2 Samuel 11:25: David was encouraged by recognizing that all persons are in similar situations. *Press the attack – say this to encourage.*

        5. Judges 20:22: In the time of battle, "But the men of Israel encouraged one another and again took up their positions where they had stationed them."

II. All who suffer with Christ have a special strength given by God. (II Corinthians 1:4)
   A. Encouragement:
      1. Share your suffering
      2. Meditate on God's Word
      3. Have faith in a positive outcome
      4. Know that God has given special strength
   B. Hoping:
      1. How To Hope:
         a. Trust in God
         b. Depend on God
         c. Rejoice because of endurance
         d. Rejoice because of the Glory of God
         e. Rejoice in God's Love
         f. Praise God because He is God
         g. Pray
         h. Be encouraged through God's Word
      2. Exercise your hoping skills if you experience the following:
         a. Feel trapped
         b. Feel lonely
         c. Feel that things will never change
         d. Feel distant from God.
         e. Feel distant from others

KEEPING HOPE ALIVE

I. During trials and times of suffering one must wait in confident expectation.

   A. Hope is a covenant relationship based on God's commitment and the believer's personal trust.

   B. This type of hope from Job 17:13-16 is patience.

II. In the New Testament Hope is always related to something good.

   A. Based on a relationship with God.

   B. The objects of hope are Jesus, The living Word,

   C. The object of hope is Scriptures, the spoken and written word.

   D. The Greek term for hope being having Favorable and confident expectation of future events.

III. Hope is reliance on the Lord, Ps. 39:7, "My hope is in You, only You can save from transgression."

   A. All who have hope can take courage.

   B. The Lord preserves the faithful (Psalm 31:23-24)

   C. Waiting on God to reveal and do what He said in His Word, Psalm 130:5-8, is hope. *This is why the Watchmen wait for the morning.*

IV. Hope is Trust, A gift from God through the action of the Holy Spirit. (Roman 15:13)

   A. *A living hopes that in spite of circumstances, we have salvation through the work of Jesus Christ.*

   B. Hope is waiting for the future events which we have not seen.

   C. Hope is the mystery that Christ is in believers regardless of nationality, origin.

Thorn In The Side[15]
Having a Spiritual and Humble Attitude.

I. Paul had a thorn, believed a physical malady, which the Lord did not remove but said, "My grace is sufficient." (II Corinthians 12:7-10)

II. God had a reason for not removing the Thorn.

    A. God wanted to guard against being puffed up.

    B. God wanted to reveal His power in a weak vessel.

    C. God wanted to teach to live for Christ's sake.

III. Paul demonstrated an attitude of love for the Corinthians by not being a burden regardless of his condition.

    A. In times of such suffering we must demonstrate love.

    B. 1 Corinthians 13:3 And if I give all my possessions to feed the [poor], and if I deliver my body to be burned, but do not have love, it profits me nothing.

        1. Love requires endurance (13:4)

        2. Love rejoices with the truth (13:6)

        3. Love bears all things, believes all things, hopes all things, endures all things. (13:7)

IV. Today's thorns in the flesh

    A. Panic attacks

    B. Unemployment

    C. Failures

    D. Physical conditions

    E. Eye Trouble

---

[15] *What the Bible Says...to The Minister,* Chattanooga, TN Leadership Ministries Worldwide. 1991, pp343-61.

COUNTING IT ALL JOY

I. Counting the trials we encounter as joy is a result of faith.

   A. The Book of James is a Book of Wisdom.

   B. The Book of James is a Book of Faith.

   C. Trials are a test of our faith.

   D. Trials prove/improve our faith.

   E. Strength can build during times of suffering.

   F. Scripture: James 1: 2-15 (Background) Key: James 1: 2-7) 1 Peter 5: 6-10

II. How to count trials as joy.

   A. Know the difference between going through a trial and having yielded to temptation.

      1. The term trial in James, is related to the Greek term, **an experiment**.

         a. Used in Hebrew 11:29 (by faith the people passed through the Red Sea...),

         b. To assay

         c. To try

      2. This term is also translated as temptations in other contexts.

      3. James explains the difference between temptations and tribulations.

         a. vv13-16 Personal lusts tempts us, and evil leads us.

         b. We give in to temptations.

         c. Trials are not a result of what we do or do not do.

         d. v15: We pay when we give in to temptations.

         e. We learn from having followed our temptations,

- f. Not the joy to which James speaks.
- g. Note: Discipline is not applicable in this context.

B. God allows us to experience trials.

1. vv 2 The key word is **when, otan, Greek meaning when, whenever, as often as, until,** not a conditional clause one of certainty.

2. Barbara Lee Johnson, "Count It All Joy", references Isaiah 43:2-3 reminds us that we will go through some trials, "when we pass through the waters, I will be with you, When you walk through the fire you will not be scorched."
   - a. Isaiah is telling Israel that God is with them
   - b. He is their Savior,
   - c. He loves them.
   - d. The believer today
   - e. He is our Savior,
   - f. He loves us. (John 3:16, 1 John 4:8-10)
   - g. The Hebrew prefix is the term when.

3. In Isaiah 43:1, God reminds Israel
   - a. He is the creator,
   - b. The redeemer,
   - c. He calls them by name.
   - d. Knowing the name denotes a special relationship.
   - e. During times of testing, do not harden your heart as did the Israelites as this is a time of molding. (Hebrew 3:7-9)

4. v3 Our faith, not our salvation, is being tested.
   - a. Know what you believe

        1'. The Gospel of Jesus Christ

        2'. The Promises of God

    b. Know Why You Believe.

        1'. The Word of God.

        2'. The Witness of The Holy Spirit.

        3'. The Witness of His Creation.

    c. Proving iron in the fire:

        1'. Get rid of impurities.

        2'. Strengthens the iron.

        3'. Under attack, your faith remained in tact.

        4'. Under attack, You accepted God's Will in the matter.

5. vv4, We must recognize that we will become more mature in Christ as we stand the test.

    a. Maturity: Fruit of the Spirit (Galatians 5: 22-26)

    b. Good Works: Fruit of our Faith (James 2:14)

6. v5 Wisdom enables one to face, endure trials, with joy.

    a. Colossians 1:9-11: Spiritual wisdom involves a knowledge of God's will.(Living worthy, strengthened by His power with joy and endurance)

        1'. Biblical wisdom: Proverbs 2:6: For the Lord gives wisdom and from His mouth come knowledge and understanding.

        2'. James 3:17: The wisdom that comes from heaven is first of all pure.

        3'. The wisdom from heaven is peace-loving.

        4'. The wisdom from heaven is considerate.

        5'. The wisdom from heaven is submissive.

- 6'. The wisdom from heaven is full of mercy
- 7'. The wisdom from heaven is full of good fruit.
- 8'. The wisdom from heaven is impartial.
- 9'. The wisdom from heaven is sincere

b. Wisdom provides the insight of the spiritual rewards of the trial. (Proverbs 1:2-4)

c. Wisdom helps us to see pure joy of our faith.

d. God will give you what is needed to get through the situation.

e. With God given wisdom, we get a different perspective of the situation.

f. "A person who approaches each decision in life with a trust in the Lord and who acknowledges God rather than leaning on his own understanding is wise. " (Richards, p. 1029)

g. Wisdom is the application of God's revelation to life rather than mere knowledge. (Ibid., p 1030)

C. Persevere with humility when under the hand of God. (James 1:2-4; 1 Peter 5:5c- 6)

1. We can consider trials joy, because our character is perfected through endurance.

2. During these trials we learn to handle situations:

   a. In humility we will receive God's Grace.

   b. Suffering becomes a source of strength. (2 Corinthians 1:4-6; 12:9)

   c. Concerns not of our control, we give to God. (1 Peter 5:7)

   d. Be Spiritual alert as Satan will seek a time of testing, suffering, to tempt you. (1 Peter 5:8)

e. Through our Faith we can resist the temptation. (1 Peter 5:9)

COMFORT

Our God is compassionate, and to endure we must know that He will comfort us. (2 Corinthians 1:3-7)

- Praise be to the God and Father of our Lord Jesus Christ, and the Father of compassion and the God of all comfort
- Who comforts us in all our troubles, so that we can comfort those in any trouble with the comfort we ourselves have received from God.
- Just as the suffering of Christ flow over into our lives, so also through Christ our comfort overflows.
- If we are distressed, it is for your comfort and salvation; if we are comforted, it is for your endurance of the same sufferings we suffer.
- And our hope for you is firm, because we know that just as you share in our sufferings, so also you share in our comfort.

The victory of Jesus Christ is spread by believers as the fragrance of a flower for those who are alive in Christ and share the victory. It is a sweet smell; but for those who remain in their sins, and have no knowledge of Christ, they can't smell the fragrance, as they are as dead. (2 Corinthians 2:11-17)

Paul's ministry was fraught with afflictions of every kind, but because his ministry is a result of God's mercy, he has hope in eternal rewards, and temporary deliverance. God takes Paul through afflictions, but not out of them. The painful episodes in Paul's ministry do not cause Paul to lose heart (2 Corinthians 4:1); Paul trusts that God will deliver him from the perils of death until the course for Jesus has been successfully run (4:8-14) (Walvoord & Zuck, 556).

Endurance of suffering is evidence of being genuine and of God's sufficiency. (2 Corinthians 11:23-13:11)

Paul is confronted by false teachers and is even attacked by members of the Corinthians Church [false brothers], and he defends his apostleship. Paul sums up his experience of 12:2-4, "Our light and momentary troubles are achieving for us an eternal glory that far outweighs them all, 4:14.

BIBLIOGRAPHY

Aland, Barbara, et al. (eds.) (1994). *The Greek New Testament,* (4th rev. ed.) German: Deutsche Bibilgesellschaft, United Bible Societies,

Alpha-Omega Ministries, (1996).*What The Bible Says...To The Minister.* Chattanooga, TN: Leadership Ministries Worldwide,

Arndt, W. F. and Gingrich F. W. (1979). *A Greek-English Lexicon of The New Testament.* (2nd Ed. Rev.) Chicago, IL: University of Chicago Press.

Berry, R. G. (1987). *Interlinear Greek-English New Testament, KJV.* Grand Rapids, Michigan: Baker Book House

Docker, D. S. (Gen. Ed.). *Holman Bible Handbook.* Nashville, TN: Holman Bible Publishers, 1986.

Martin, R. P. (1986). *Word Biblical Commentary 2 Corinthians.* Waco TX: Word Books Publishers,

Radmacher, E. D. (Gen. Ed.) *The Nelson Study Bible, NKJV.* Nashville, TN: Thomas Nelson Publishers, 1989.

Richards, L. O. (1987). *The Teacher's Commentary.* Wheaton, IL: Victor Books,

Richards, L. O. (1991). *New International Encyclopedia of Bible Words.* Grand Rapids, MI: Zondervan Publishing House,

Scofield, C.I. (ED). *The New Scofield Bible, NKJV.* Nashville: Thomas Nelson, 1989.

Thompson, F. C. (1979). *The Thompson Chain-Reference Bible, NASB.* Indianapolis, IN: Lockman Foundation.

Vine, W.E., Unger, M. F., and White, W. (1985). *Vine's Complete Expository Dictionary of Old and New Testament Words.* Nashville, TN: Thomas Nelson Publishers.

Walvoord, J. F. and Luck, R. B. (1983). *The Bible Knowledge Commentary, New Testament.* Based on NIV, Chariot: Victory Publishers,

Wiersbe, Warren W. *Be Encouraged.* USA: Victor Books, 1988.

Williams, J. (2000). *Sheep In Wolves Clothing.* Chicago, IL: Moody Press.

SERMONS

Jackson, Brenda Simuel. (2000). "Be Strengthened," Wayne County Jail,

Jackson, Brenda Simuel. (2004). "Count It All Joy," Scott's Correctional Facility,

PAPERS

Jackson, B. S. "Encouragement and Joy During Fateful Affliction and Faithful"

"Suffering," An Analysis of Themes of Comfort and Encouragement in Second Corinthian, Philippians, and Second Timothy. Theology, Plymouth, MI December 1, 1997.

ABOUT THE AUTHOR

Brenda Simuel Jackson (BA, MA, Master of Divinity, Ph.D.), is a born again Christian, affiliated with the Baptist Faith. She is a member and Minister of New Prospect Missionary Baptist Church, and does ministry through BSJ Christian Seminars, Inc. (501) (c) (3), a Prison/Jail Ministry, an outreach and equipment ministry. She is a graduate of Wayne State University, and Michigan Theological Seminary. She is a member of the Pulpit Ministry, assists in the Teaching, Prison ministries and intercessory Prayer Ministry of her church. She has over thirty years of experience in human Services, education administration, and management, as well as part-time collegiate instruction. She is currently a part-time faculty member of Wayne County Community College District. She has presented at Conferences of the American Association of Christian Counselors,' at local Church Women's retreats, and Mission programs, At Christian Education Institutes, at State Correctional Facilities, and Professional and Community Programs.

Her Christian Journey includes short term outreach mission assignments in Japan, South Africa, and Jamaica. Her goals include future short term mission as God so directs. She is a widow, a mother, a grandmother, the ninth child of Willie and Lucy Simuel (both deceased). She is a native Detroiter. Dr. Jackson is a called minister of the Gospel, and was endorsed for Chaplaincy clergy by the National Baptist Convention, USA, Inc. Home Mission Board in June 2004.

Dr. Jackson is also a published writer who released her first book entitled, *A Journey of Redeeming Faith*, in April 2007, her second book entitled, *Being Wonderfully Made*, in September 2008 and now this volume, her third book entitled, *Going Through*. These are the first three seminar compilations in her series entitled *Reflections on the Path to Wholeness*. Dr. Jackson has also hosted a radio broadcast, "God's Teaching Moments."

Her Christian Journey includes short term outreach mission in Japan, South Africa (multiple visits), and Jamaica. She is scheduled for prison ministry in South Africa, in January 2009, and in Ghana in August 2009.

She is a member of The Daughters of Deborah, The Council of Baptist Pastors of Detroit and Vicinity, Christian Professional and Business Women's Association, and the American Association of Christian Counselors. She is an Alpha Kappa Alpha woman, a certified teacher for the Sunday School Publishing Board and a licensed Minister of the Gospel. Her vineyard is the prisons of the world.

BOOK ORDER FORM

Reflections on the Path to Wholeness: Vol 1

A Journey of Redeeming Faith

By Brenda S. Jackson, Ph.D.

Name _____

Address _____

City _____ State _____ Zip _____

Phone _____ Fax _____

Email _____

Quantity		
Price *(each)*		$9.99
Subtotal		
S & H *(each)*		$1.99
MI Tax 6%		
TOTAL		

METHOD OF PAYMENT:

☐ Check or Money Order (*Make payable to*: **PriorityONE Publications**)

☐ Visa   ☐ Master Card   ☐ American Express

Acct No. _____

Expiration Date (*mmyy*) _____

Signature _____

Mail your payment with this form to:
PriorityONE Publications
P. O. Box 725
Farmington, MI 48332
(800) 596-4490 – Toll Free
URL: http://www.p1pubs.com
Email: info@p1pubs.com

BOOK ORDER FORM

Reflections on the Path to Wholeness: Vol 2

Being *Wonderfully* Made
By Brenda S. Jackson, Ph.D.

Name _____

Address _____

City _____ State _____ Zip _____

Phone _____ Fax _____

Email _____

Quantity	
Price *(each)*	$11.99
Subtotal	
S & H *(each)*	$1.99
MI Tax 6%	
TOTAL	

METHOD OF PAYMENT:

☐ Check or Money Order (*Make payable to*: PriorityONE Publications)

☐ Visa   ☐ Master Card   ☐ American Express

Acct No. _____

Expiration Date (*mmyy*) _____

Signature _____

Mail your payment with this form to:
PriorityONE Publications
P. O. Box 725
Farmington, MI 48332
(800) 596-4490 – Toll Free
URL: http://www.p1pubs.com
Email: info@p1pubs.com

BOOK ORDER FORM

Reflections on the Path to Wholeness: Vol 3

Going Through

By Brenda S. Jackson, Ph.D.

Name _____

Address _____

City _____ State _____ Zip _____

Phone _____ Fax _____

Email _____

Quantity	
Price *(each)*	$11.99
Subtotal	
S & H *(each)*	$1.99
MI Tax 6%	
TOTAL	

METHOD OF PAYMENT:

☐ Check or Money Order (*Make payable to*: PriorityONE Publications)

☐ Visa   ☐ Master Card   ☐ American Express

Acct No. _____

Expiration Date (*mmyy*) _____

Signature _____

Mail your payment with this form to:
PriorityONE Publications
P. O. Box 725
Farmington, MI 48332
(800) 596-4490 – Toll Free
URL: http://www.p1pubs.com
Email: info@p1pubs.com

www.ingramcontent.com/pod-product-compliance
Lightning Source LLC
Chambersburg PA
CBHW052032070526
44584CB00016B/2004